TO JOANN -

You put the 'Q' in my QTR.

TABLE OF CONTENTS

QUALITY
TIME
REMAINING

STEVE BAKER

This publication is designed to provide competent and reliable information regarding the subject matter covered. However, it is sold with the understanding that the author and publisher are not engaged in rendering legal, financial, or other professional advice. Laws and practices often vary from state to state and country to country and if expert assistance is required, the services of a professional should be sought. The author and publisher specifically disclaim any liability that is incurred from the use or application of the contents of this book.

WARNING: Face it. You probably won't do this. This is not for everyone. This is for less than 3% of our population who are willing to go from wish to vision to goal to execution. The secret is discipline and frequency. You will need accountability. The mental game is the hardest, so remember to fight your programming and limiting beliefs. Good luck on your journey!

For Additional Copies of Quality Time Remaining™ and the Complete QTR™ Workbook, Visit QTRbook.com

Published by QTR, LLC.

No Artificial Intelligence was used in the writing of this book

Printed in the United States of America

ISBN: 979-8-9899524-0-3 (Hardcover)
ISBN: 979-8-9899524-1-0 (eBook)
ISBN: 979-8-9899524-2-7 (Softcover)

Book Design and Illustrations by Colin Baker and Steve Baker

QTRBK120124

TABLE OF CONTENTS

01. INTRODUCTION

You Only Live Once, But if You Do it Right, Once is Enough.

Mae West
1893–1980

01. INTRODUCTION

Do you remember what you were doing October 30th of 2018?

If you're like me, you were probably buying Halloween candy.

A lot of things were going on for us that year. Life was good. I'm a lucky man. Incredible kids, gorgeous wife, meaningful work. I was having a great time. JoAnn and I had just celebrated our 29th wedding anniversary. We had just seen *A Star Is Born* the weekend before, and I was halfway through writing the definitive "how-to" book on open-book management. That afternoon, we all went as a family to take homecoming photos with our youngest son.

I was good! Work was good, home was good. October 30th, 2018 was also the day that we heard these words:

Stage 3 Prostate Cancer.

Aw, come on! Is *this* the kind of book it's gonna be?

NO. I'm trying to make a point.

That's life. Everything's going great, then something gets hurled at you. That's just the way things go. The question is, what will you do? Do you have the personal resilience to not only survive, but thrive in modern life?

Let's go back to cancer for a second. The five-hour robotic surgery was a success. Within a few weeks, I was back on the road, coast-to-coast, speaking to the largest audiences of my career. Things were happening again!

In the following months, we finished the book. I went into the studio to record it for Audible. JoAnn and I celebrated our 30th wedding anniversary. We had a great family vacation. Nine months flew by. And then around Labor Day, I learned my PSA was back.

PSA, or prostate-specific antigen, is a protein produced by the cells of the prostate gland. If you own a prostate and you've not had it checked, do it *today*. Wait, since I no longer had a prostate, where was this marker coming from? As it happens, malignant cells *also* produce PSA, and my doctors ramped up for the next level of treatment.

As I write this, I feel as though there are a lot of people out there thinking about my groin right now. Let's get back on track.

The standard of care at that point was 40 rounds of radiation plus hormone treatment.

When I heard this, I was not happy. Radical prostatectomy has, let's just say, some *unpleasant* side effects. Side effects that I was just getting used to; I didn't need *more*. The drug they use is called Lupron®. Lupron very effectively starves cancer cells by removing all testosterone from your body. Testosterone is like rocket fuel for cancer. And for me, the side effects of Lupron lasted 18 months.

I wasn't ready for *any* of them. Here's the list of side effects directly from the manufacturer, AbbVie®. I was spared only one. You're going to have to guess which one it was.

I gained 35 pounds. I couldn't sleep at night. I was on edge. I couldn't remember where I parked. Every joint hurt. I couldn't even make a fist. I started a nation-wide tour to apologize to every woman in my life over the age of 50, because hot flashes are real, and they suck. JoAnn told me I was going through '*Man-opause*'.

I didn't think of it this way at the time, but it was a gift. All these horrible side effects were a preview to old age. And it made it very clear to me that I did not want to age this way. I was going to do something about it. I began to realize that in America, the scariest thing is not to die. The scariest thing is to live very sick, for a very long time.

I had to realign my priorities around what was most important.

Luckily, I had an ace in the hole. I asked my daughter's pre-ancé (that's our family's term for pre-fiancé), Will, to tell me the day I was going to die.

You see, Will is an actuary.

Will and his firm advise companies with pension plans by valuing the financial costs, risks, and uncertainties of lifetime income after retirement. They are always forecasting, well, people stuff. Since he is telling companies how long their employee populations are going to live, it seemed logical that the actuaries could put some science to a spreadsheet I've had for years. Essentially a matrix of my age against all the important people, events, and things in my life.

This spreadsheet goes from today to age 106. There was no science there. 106 columns just happened to be how many fit on a printed 11x17 sheet of paper.

It includes items like JoAnn, the kids, their significant others (they call themselves Sig-O's). Next come our parents, siblings, pets, even the house and cars. The spreadsheet was designed to help me grapple with questions like "How long will we have Mom and Dad? When do you think the kids will have kids? How long will these student loans go?"

'Will the Actuary' gave me the science I needed to get what I wanted in the time I actually had left.

A PREVIEW TO OLD AGE

Now, you might believe that October 30, 2018 was the day that

Quality Time Remaining was born. It wasn't. QTR was born the following year, Fall 2019, a couple of months into Lupron treatment.

One fine Fall Saturday morning, I'd crawled under the kitchen sink to check a fitting on our garbage disposal. When I finished, I could not get off the floor of my kitchen. Basically, I had fallen and I couldn't get up.

That was the day QTR was born.

That October morning, lying on the floor, I realized I was basically 90 years old because of the drug. Is this what I had to look forward to? No way! *That* is the day I knew I had something to share. I'd had a sneak peek at what life might be like if I didn't take action right away.

As we now get into the tenets and tools that make up Quality Time Remaining, I want you to remember this:

QTR will help you pinpoint exactly who you are, what you want, and how to get it in the time that you have left.

THE PROMISE:
QTR will not solve your problems.

THE GUARANTEE:
Practiced with discipline and frequency, QTR will help you achieve a higher *quality* of life, and very possibly increase your longevity.

QTR is not about gloom and doom. It's not about 'when am I going to die?' It's about freedom. Freedom from anxiety and fear. Freedom from all the unnecessary conflict, suffering, and drama we throw into our lives, or that we accept from other people. Freedom from the excuses, procrastination, and resistance that prevent us from focusing on the things you want most from life.

According to the Bureau of Labor Statistics, the average person will spend thirty percent of their life sleeping, thirty percent going to school and working, twenty percent eating, shopping, child-rearing, commuting. Twelve percent will be flushed on TV, video games and social media. What's left? Eight percent? Roughly 6 years left to...live. *That's unacceptable.*

Quality Time Remaining is about living instead of just surviving. It's about designing a life instead of making a living. QTR looks at every area of your life, every facet of your being - Mindset, Physical, Financial, Relationships, Spiritual, Career and Legacy - all of it. Then, helps you bring each into focus.

QTR gives you permission to focus and permission to win in life; to give you the highest quality of life in the limited time you have left.

Until now, there hasn't been a simple set of instructions. And that, my friends, is what Quality Time Remaining is all about. You're gonna need a system.

02. THE FOUR TENETS OF QTR

A Bad System Will Beat a Good Person Every Time.

W. Edwards Deming
1900–1993

02. THE FOUR TENETS OF QTR

These are the four tenets of Quality Time Remaining.

Embrace Mortality
Amplify Objectivity
Choose Growth
Accept Happiness

The first is we've got to embrace our mortality. Life doesn't last forever; what do we have left? It's not a negative. It's just data.

Second, we need to gain objectivity about where we are in life today. Becoming objective allows us to then subjectively decide what we want to accomplish in the time we have left. You can't do it all, so you must opt for only that which is most important to us.

Third, you must choose growth over decay. This is a big one.

Finally, something you probably haven't thought a lot about. You will have to give yourself permission to accept your own happiness and satisfaction. Many of us don't. We put ourselves last, and it's time we changed that.

Let's look at these one at a time.

Embrace Mortality
Amplify Objectivity
Choose Growth
Accept Happiness

EMBRACE MORTALITY

The first tenet is to embrace our mortality. While many of us think we want to live forever, that's not possible, and probably not wise. We must make the most of what we've got.

How much time do you have right now?

Remember "Will the Actuary"? Will the Actuary helped me design the QTR Life Expectancy Chart, based on the actual mortality experienced by pension plans and projected trends in the United States*. Just find your age in the Chart below and the number next to it. In the illustration, for example, look at age 59. Next to it, you can see the number 26.2. That's the QTR number. If you are 29 years old, 55.3 is your QTR number. Now, circle your own age and the adjacent QTR number, then insert the current year, your QTR number and total them in the boxes below.

Age	QTR	Age	QTR	Age	QTR	Age	QTR	Age	QTR	Age	QTR
20	64.2	30	54.3	40	44.4	50	34.7	60	25.2	70	16.7
21	63.2	31	53.3	41	43.5	51	33.7	61	24.3	71	16.0
22	62.2	32	52.3	42	42.5	52	32.7	62	23.5	72	15.2
23	61.2	33	51.3	43	41.5	53	31.8	63	22.6	73	14.4
24	60.2	34	50.3	44	40.5	54	30.8	64	21.7	74	13.7
25	59.2	35	49.4	45	39.5	55	29.9	65	20.9	75	12.9
26	58.2	36	48.4	46	38.6	56	28.9	66	20.0	76	12.2
27	57.2	37	47.4	47	37.6	57	28.0	67	19.2	77	11.5
28	56.3	38	46.4	48	36.6	58	27.1	68	18.4	78	10.8
29	55.3	39	45.4	49	35.6	59	26.2	69	17.5	79	10.2

This Year		My QTR		QTR Year	Probability
	+		=		

*Source: IRC 430 (h) (3) (A)

Do I have your attention?

For some, this will be a shock. For others, not so much. I had a 28-year-old creative tell me, "56 years? That's probably too long...". I literally laughed out loud. Most people look sad and perplexed, "Is that it? For real?"

What feelings come up for you?

In live events, people will fight with me saying, "I was born in a Blue Zone!" (I wasn't), "I'm a triathlete!" (I'm not), or "My Great Aunt Nita lived to be 106!" (mine did). This just means I have their attention.

Can you make the number go up? Sure! Start eating right, exercising, getting enough sleep, and sell your motorcycle. Can you make the number go down? Absolutely! Grab a pack of smokes and a bottle of scotch on your way to skydiving classes.

How close do you need your number to be?

Google returns 74,600,000 results to the query 'life expectancy calculator'. There are so many great ones out there, many of which are completely free. GO USE ONE! *Living to 100* is one of my personal favorites. Today, you can also pay a service that will use your DNA to calculate a more precise date, and even your biological age. There is no lack of resources in this arena. Find something that makes you want to take action.

We're just looking to put a stake in the ground. This is the number. So how does it feel? It's probably a bit of a shock, isn't it?

Now it's time for the bonus round.

As I was thanking Will the Actuary for his help in developing the QTR Life Expectancy Chart, he said, "You know you're not done yet, right?" Taken aback, I stammered, "There's more?"

"These are life *expectancies*. No matter your age, there is a 50% chance that you'll live fewer years, and a 50% chance you'll live more years." Ouch. That really got my attention. Now you know what the 4th gray box is, marked "Probability". Just write "50%" in that box. Aren't actuaries dreamy?

The U.S. Government thinks you're going to live to be about 86 if you're a healthy female, and respectively 83 years old if you're a male. Those life expectancies come directly from the Social Security Administration. I am personally not satisfied by that, and of course you have a lot of sway over which side of that number you're going to land on.

If you are a visual learner like me, check out Tim Urban's 'Wait But Why' website at *www.waitbutwhy.com*. He's known for a visual he came up with called 'your life in weeks'. I'm partial to his 'your life in months' that looks something like this:

In this example, a 39 year old has filled in 39 of 83 years. What does yours look like? Does this visual give you more perspective than just a number?

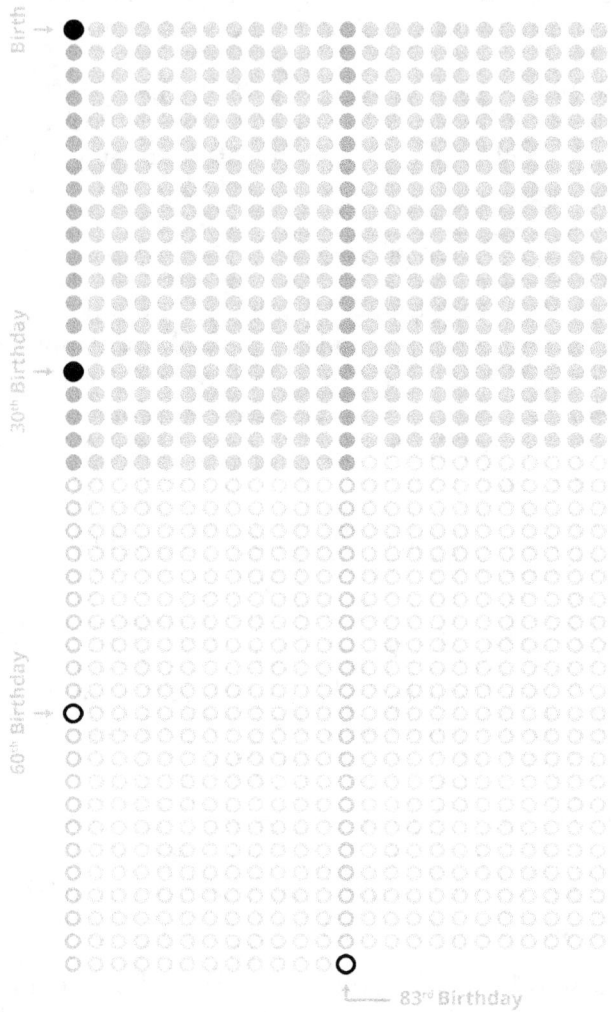

Adapted from Tim Urban's waitbutwhy.com

What's the point of all this?

It's to get you out of the 'I've got plenty of time' mindset and into one of urgency, gratitude, and purpose. Remember, knowing how long the game will last can radically change how you play it.

Now that I have your attention, let's take it to the next level, and talk about amplifying your newfound objectivity.

Embrace Mortality
Amplify Objectivity
Choose Growth
Accept Happiness

AMPLIFY OBJECTIVITY

Embracing your mortality might take some adjustment. Remember, we're trying to get comfortable with the idea that you won't be here forever.

Next, you want to look objectively at not only your own timeline, but at the most meaningful people, events and things around you. Looking at your QTR number, does it change anything about how you make decisions?

> *"Knowing how long the game will last can radically change the way you play it."*
>
> *Steve Baker*

Maybe it's about fixing that relationship you've been avoiding for years. Or perhaps it's about putting some money away for retirement or paying down student loan debt. Maybe it's actually retiring. Whatever it is, I hope you see it coming into focus.

To help you do this, we'll use the QTR Timeline Assessment.

The QTR Timeline Assessment

The Timeline Assessment is inspired by the 106 column spreadsheet I mentioned earlier. On the left axis, you'll list the names important to you. Yourself, your 'Sig-O', children, their Sig-O's, then who else? Your parents, grandparents, grandchildren, close friends, pets...I even put big things like the house, the cars, the A/C unit...anything that will help you 'see the matrix' over the coming years. It's really impactful to plot this out to your full QTR age in a spreadsheet of your own, but for now, we'll work with only the next 10 years.

You should now have the left axis filled in. From left to right, you will now write the age of each line item, from today through the next 10 years. Are you starting to see the connections?

Plot the Ages of Key Relationships on the Timeline Below.

Years from Today	1	2	3	4	5	6	7	8	9	10
Self										
Sig-O										
Child										
Sig-O										
Who Else?										
Who Else?										
Who Else?										
Who Else?										

Someone at a live event recently challenged my logic in putting things like pets and cars into the timeline. Consider this. Our little dog, Snickers, is JoAnn's close companion. With me on the road constantly, and Snickers being 14 at the time of this writing, shouldn't I be thinking about it? Our dog has already outlived her warranty! What will we do when she's gone?

In 10 years, JoAnn's father will be 107, and he's just ornery enough to make it! How will that impact our lives?

Our kids are at the age where they'll be getting engaged, married, and starting careers. I want to be there for all of it!

Again, it's not about being negative or morose. Facing difficult situations before they arrive takes the bite out of them and returns power from the situation back to you.

Author Nassim Nicholas Taleb says in his book *Antifragile* "Invest in prepared-ness, not prediction." In business, we teach entrepreneurs how to use contingency plans; prepare for the worst... expect the best.

The Stoics called this *premeditatio malorum.* They would regularly contemplate all the things that could go awry or be taken away in life. This worst-case scenario thinking helped them prepare for, and become more resilient to, life's inevitable setbacks. This exercise is your first foray into becoming anti-fragile and ready for anything. It's really quite freeing.

Personally, I don't consider worst-case thinking as negative at all. I choose to use it to plan ahead. One woman I met told me it was instrumental in her own wellness regimen. She wanted to be able to run and play with her grandchildren well into her 80's. She was 40 at the time.

Spend time with the QTR Timeline. Play with it. Model it out a number of ways. You'll start to see how valuable the exercise can be. If you're bold, you'll layout your own 100 year spreadsheet and take back your power. It'll open your eyes!

Next, we'll talk about the most important decision you can make.

Embrace Mortality
Amplify Objectivity
Choose Growth
Accept Happiness

CHOOSE GROWTH

In life, everything is subject to entropy. The second law of thermodynamics (in layman's terms) states that a closed system will fall into decay without the addition of additional energy. Left unchecked, disorder increases over time and systems dissolve into chaos. In one form or another, entropy is everywhere. Overlook regular home maintenance, and the place will fall apart. Don't stress your body with exercise, and you'll be more susceptible to illness and disease. Stuff your money into your mattress instead of an interest-bearing account, and inflation will eat away at the value of your stash. Ignore your most important relationships, and well, you know what happens then.

> *"The most basic human impulse is towards entropy & laziness."*
> *Alexandra Fuller*
> *b. 1969*

Life doesn't stand still, and neither can you.

In this life, you don't have two choices – growth or decay. You only have *one* choice: Growth. Because if you're not growing, you're decaying. Throughout QTR, you'll be presented with a series of Challenges that will help you wrestle with the growth you want, and the decay you allow into your life.

Remember to always be looking for small ways to keep entropy at bay and keep growing in positive ways. You will hit obstacles and roadblocks. One of the biggest you'll encounter is YOU. Then you'll have to learn to accept your own happiness and satisfaction.

Embrace Mortality
Amplify Objectivity
Choose Growth
Accept Happiness

ACCEPT HAPPINESS

The fourth tenet of Quality Time Remaining is to learn to accept your own happiness and satisfaction. Believe it or not, most people (short of narcissists and sociopaths) have a hard time allowing themselves to be happy and satisfied. Where do you fall along that spectrum? I am a lifelong people pleaser and 'fixer'. It takes a great deal of resolve for me to stop finding more problems to fix, and stay in the moment to savor some of the happiest moments life can offer.

The first step in accepting happiness is to identify what makes you happy. What is it that you want out of life? That's more difficult to answer than you thought, isn't it? Today, most people have a very hard time answering these two questions:

Who are you, and what do you want?

Modern life has actually made it incredibly difficult to choose what you want, because of choice overload. There's just too much to choose from!

In *The Paradox of Choice*, psychologist Barry Schwartz writes about Hick's Law, which states that the time it takes to make a decision increases with the number of choices. We all know that the more choices there are, the harder it is to decide. If you don't believe me, go find something on Netflix to watch tonight. This is a perfect way to find yourself in 'analysis paralysis', leaving you with no decision made and feeling miserable.

Later, we'll be using a QTR tool designed to help you decide what you want. For the moment, would it be safe to say that the first thing you want for yourself and the people you care about is to 'be happy'? It's a pretty good guess, considering there are currently over 23,000 books in print on happiness.

Want to know what the #1 predictor of happiness is?

It's not the new job, fast car, trophy spouse, or pile of cash we all see in movies and social media.

Let's look at two important studies on human happiness, the longest and the biggest. Robert Waldinger and Mark Schultz's *The Good Life: Lessons from the*

Longest Scientific Study on Happiness summarizes the Harvard Study of Adult Development. "The simple but surprising answer is: relationships. The stronger our relationships, the more likely we are to live happy, satisfying, and healthier lives." The study has been tracking the lives of 724 participants for 79 years. That's a long study. But it's not the biggest.

Dr. Angus Campbell from the University of Michigan, studied nearly 6,000 participants. Campbell discovered, "Having a strong sense of controlling one's life is a more dependable predictor of positive feelings of well-being than any of the objective conditions of life we have considered." The study goes on to point out that 85% of Americans do not feel a sense of agency, autonomy or control in their lives. Yikes. Do you?

Big takeaway from these two studies? We should be working on our own internal locus of control as well as our relationships.

Another way to pursue happiness might be asking, "how much is enough?" In Sweden, the term 'lagom' is used to describe "just enough" or "just right". The Danish say 'hygge' to describe a sense of contentment and well-being. In 1947, the father of artificial intelligence, Herbert Simon, coined the term "satisfice". In other words, to satisfy and suffice is to 'satisfice'. In medicine, doctors refer to the 'minimum effective dose', as more is not always better. In software, 'minimum viable product' or MVP refers to an early release with only the features required to satisfy the test audience in order to get feedback that informs the next generation of the product. In life, we might look for the minimum satisfactory condition or outcome, rather than killing ourselves to find elusive perfection.

> ## *"Satisfy + Suffice = Satisfice"*
> ### *Herbert A. Simon*
> #### *1916-2001*

Hold on a minute. Didn't I just lecture you about growth? Yup. I sure did. Happiness is relative, and it's temporary. Satisfaction, as opposed to happiness, is sustainable. Why not create a life of continuous improvement and satisfaction? You have to find that balance for yourself.

Dave Ramsey can be polarizing, but there's undeniable wisdom in the phrase "It's time to stop buying things we can't afford, with money we don't have, to impress people we don't like." How much is enough for you? Whose dream are you chasing? Does your happiness depend on someone else's?

My heart's wish for you is to live a life of *your* design, to know who *you* are, and get what *you* want, in the time *you* have left. That's QTR.

But what if you can't figure out what you really want?

Lucky you. I have discovered a great way to figure out what you want. It's by figuring out what you *don't* want first.

03. WHAT DO YOU WANT?

PART ONE

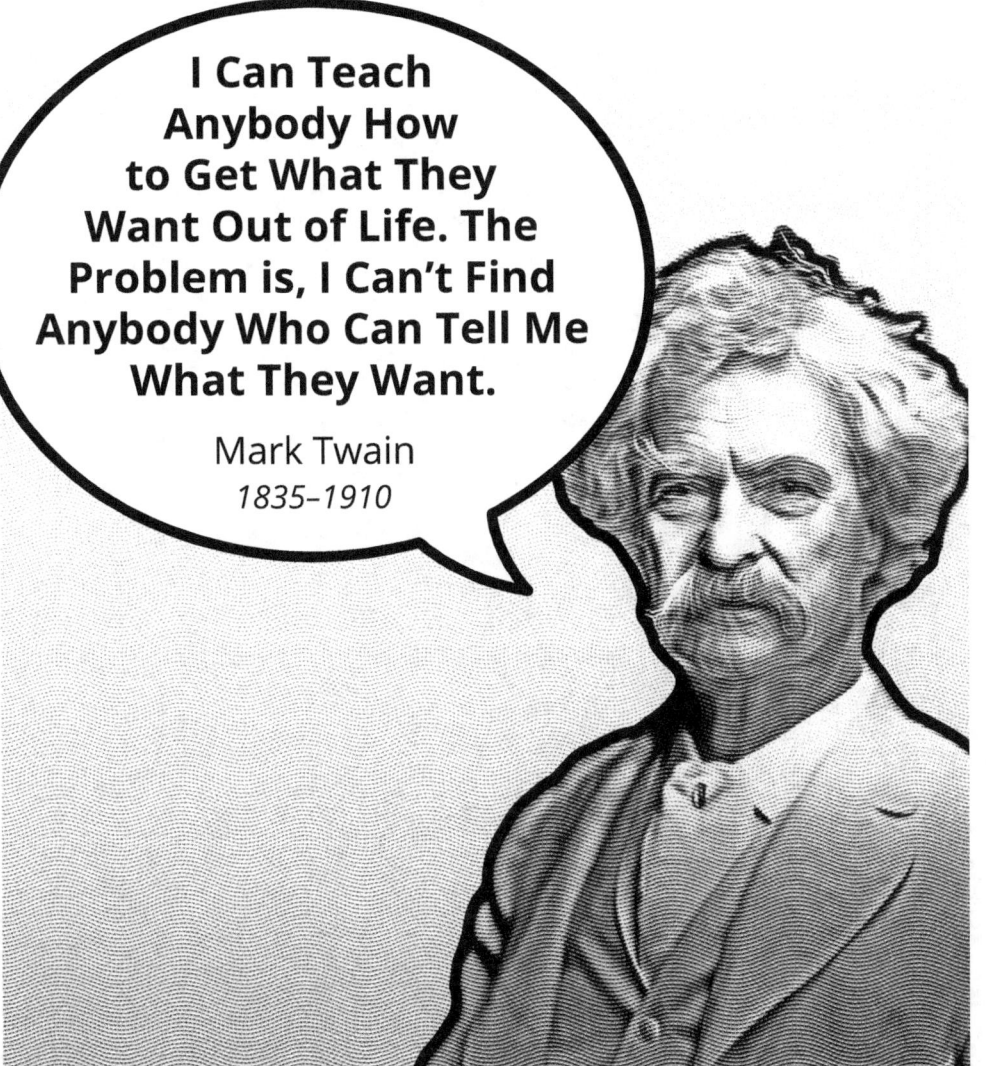

I Can Teach Anybody How to Get What They Want Out of Life. The Problem is, I Can't Find Anybody Who Can Tell Me What They Want.

Mark Twain
1835–1910

03. WHAT DO YOU WANT?

PART ONE: QTR DEFAULT FUTURE ASSESSMENT

Now that you're familiar with the four tenets of QTR, let's put them to work. We must embrace our mortality, get objective about the people and things in our lives, choose growth over decay, and become aware that we must learn to accept our own happiness and satisfaction.

It's usually at this point in live events that people start to question what matters most to them, what their priorities should be, and what they really want.

By looking at ourselves over time, we can project what might happen to us if we change nothing. Remember '*premeditatio malorum*'? The Default Future Assessment is a modern day take on that ancient Stoic practice.

Let's break life into 6 key facets:

Mindset,

Physical,

Financial,

Relationships,

Spiritual, and

Career/Legacy.

Using the QTR Default Future Assessment, write down a simple description of your life, only one year from today, if you don't change a thing. This is pretty easy, as you can imagine your life, health, family, friends, and work in a year's time. Will there be changes? Yes. Will they all be earth shattering? Probably not.

When you complete the five-year QTR Default Future Assessment, it gets a bit more challenging. Imagining those same facets across sixty months can be unnerving if you're honest with yourself. Remember, for this exercise, we're trying to imagine the worst-case scenario, assuming we change nothing.

We get set in our ways. The weight starts to pack on. Debt piles up. Relationships sour. People pass away. If we're not paying attention, we can become rudderless, drifting from one day to the next on autopilot.

The ten-year exercise can be truly revealing. Babies become teenagers. Children become adults. We get older and things hurt. Nuisances become chronic conditions. Entropy and atrophy become glaringly obvious. As you're doing this exercise, remember that we're trying to imagine the worst outcomes to inspire us to want more, to be more and to take control of our lives in every aspect.

What is possible if you don't pay attention? What does 'default' really look like? What will it cost you if changes aren't made? Visualize what that life looks like, what it feels like. What are you not saying? What is too hard to imagine?

By getting this down on paper, you're taking some of the 'scary' out of it. This can be your first step in taking back the power that time can snatch away from you. Go into each of these – the one, five and ten year assessments – with courage and honesty. The level of detail you put into these exercises will inform the richness of the results of the rest of the QTR approach.

You may feel a bit of resistance building up. I urge you to press on, because leaving it all to luck just isn't an option. Roman philosopher Seneca said it best. (Sorry Oprah fans, he said it first.)

> *"Luck is what happens when preparation meets opportunity."*
> *Lucius Annaeus Seneca*
> *d. 65 AD*

Keep in mind, it's not a negative exercise! Document those parts of your life that are going well, too. By identifying what you don't want, and what your non-negotiables in life are, you can set boundaries and goals to create the life you want... and deserve.

Get to it.

QTR DEFAULT FUTURE ASSESSMENT

For each facet of your life, describe your life **one year from today**, if you do not change a thing:

Mindset:

Physical:

Financial:

Relationships:

Spiritual:

Career/Legacy:

It's possible that your life one year from now might not look a lot different than today. This next one is going to be a little harder to swallow.

Now, describe your life **five years from today**, if you change nothing.

Mindset:

Physical:

Financial:

Relationships:

Spiritual:

Career/Legacy:

I'm guessing that you're starting to get the picture.

Next, take extra time to honestly describe each facet of your life **a full decade from today**. This exercise is for your eyes only. Be frank and honest with yourself.

Mindset:

Physical:

Financial:

Relationships:

Spiritual:

Career/Legacy:

If your relationship is the big issue in ten years, what will you do *today* to try and salvage or improve it?

If your career isn't taking you where you want to go, what are you willing to try to change it?

The Default Future Assessment is designed to highlight those things that don't seem like a big deal today, but could gain monstrous proportions over time.

Look at what you've written. In one year, carrying 10 or 15 extra pounds isn't a problem. You're busy. I get it. Five and ten years from now (if not addressed in the short term) could become diabetes, cancer, heart disease, hypertension, insomnia... do I need to go on?

Maybe the stress of student loans is nagging at you late at night or limiting you from doing the things that are most important to you. You don't want to wake up in five years with an ulcer and twenty-five years to go.

If you're operating on autopilot every day, these things will fester and insidiously creep into your life with ever-increasing impact and consequences. Take just one step to improve your own agency and control over your life, and you'll immediately increase your happiness and satisfaction.

Considering what you've captured above, can you identify one single thing you could do that would have the biggest impact on your life...in one, five, even ten years?

When I was a kid, my Grandpa Baker taught me to always eat my least favorite thing first, saving my favorite for last. Mark Twain used to say, "If it's your job to eat a frog, it's best to do it first thing in the morning. And if it's your job to eat two frogs, it's best to eat the biggest one first." You just ate the big frog. Let's look at your future from a different perspective now.

04. WHAT DO YOU WANT?

PART TWO

The Best Way to Predict Your Future is to Create it.

Peter Drucker
1909–2005

QTR PREFERRED FUTURE ASSESSMENT

Yup, you guessed it! This is the fun part; the complete opposite of the torturous exercises you just completed. For each facet of your life, describe your life **one year from today**, as you would most like to experience it.

Mindset:

Physical:

Financial:

Relationships:

Spiritual:

Career/Legacy:

QTR PREFERRED FUTURE ASSESSMENT

Next, for each facet of your life, describe your life **five years from today**, as you would most like to experience it.

Mindset:

Physical:

Financial:

Relationships:

Spiritual:

Career/Legacy:

QTR PREFERRED FUTURE ASSESSMENT

Finally, for each facet of your life, describe your life **ten years from today**, as you would most like to experience it.

Mindset:

Physical:

Financial:

Relationships:

Spiritual:

Career/Legacy:

Considering what you've captured above, can you identify one single thing you could do that would have the biggest impact on your life...in one, five, even ten years?

The QTR Default and Preferred Future Assessments should have helped you identify some of the bright spots in your life and see some of the challenges you need to face in coming months and years.

'You can't hit a target you can't see', as the old adage goes. *Knowing* what you want makes all the difference in *getting* what you want. Quality Time Remaining is all about knowing who you are, what you want and how to get it in the time you have left.

05. MAKING TIME
FOR WHAT MATTERS MOST

You Will Never
'Find' Time for
Anything. If You Want
Time, You Must Make it.

Charles Buxton
1822–1871

05. MAKING TIME
FOR WHAT MATTERS MOST

In the last two exercises, you identified a few things you would prefer in your life, and a lot of things you truly don't want in your life. It's a powerful exercise because you can give yourself a little room to dream. "What's possible? How would I feel if *this* was in my life, and *that* was out?"

The problem is, there will never be enough time in the day, week, or year to fit in all of the good stuff. You're going to have to prioritize things.

A great way to take each of the facets of life you just worked on, and put them into a timeless classic: The Wheel of Life.

QTR LIFE WHEEL

The 'Wheel of Life' is a life-planning tool that was developed in 1960's by Paul J. Meyer and widely popularized by motivational gurus like Zig Ziglar in the 1970's and Tony Robbins in the 1980's. It's not new. In fact, a quick search returns a whopping 900,000,000 results on that term alone.

The idea is simple. You put the different aspects of your life around a wheel, rate yourself on how you think you're doing in each area, then connect the dots. For instance, you might rate yourself high on your Career and Financial, but your Relationships and Spiritual are lacking. Or maybe you're struggling with money, which might affect Mindset, Financial, Physical and certainly Relationships.

In either example, your 'wheel' is out of balance. You'd have a 'flat', leaving you stranded and suffering on the shoulder of life's highway.

I've identified 6 facets, because I like simple. (Simple gets *done*.) You worked on these in the last chapter:

Mindset,

Physical,

Financial,

Relationships,

Spiritual,

Career/Legacy.

Mindset because that's where your life begins. Physical because if you don't feel good, the rest of your life is impacted. Financial because it funds everything. Relationships because that's what life is all about. Spiritual because regardless of your system of beliefs, faith will get you through the toughest times. And Career if you are on the younger side; Legacy might be what you're thinking about if you're more senior.

> *"Things which matter most must never be at the mercy of things which matter least."*
> *Stephen R. Covey*
> *1932-2012*

When I first started teaching QTR to live audiences, I got a real variety of responses to the Wheel of Life. The most common response was, "You should start with..." then fill in the blank. For some audiences, it was Spiritual. For others, Physical. Some said Relationships. Guess what? They're right. They're ALL right.

Remember, IT'S A WHEEL! TURN THE WHEEL! You should start with the facet of life that is right for you.

As I pointed out before, this wheel idea is not new. I don't want to re-invent the wheel, I want to *evert* it.

That's right, evert it. To evert is to turn inside out. Much like Copernicus did in 1543, when he everted Ptolemy's theory that the sun revolved around the Earth. Eversion is important, because I want to turn the wheel of life inside out, putting your Quality Time Remaining at the very center of your life.

In the QTR Life Wheel exercise, you'll first write your QTR years remaining or your QTR year in the center of the wheel. Then rate yourself 1 to 5 in each facet of your life. 1 being worst, 5 being best. Once you've plotted dots in each facet, connect the dots. Where are you out of balance? What's lacking in your life? Where are you excelling?

Here's an example:

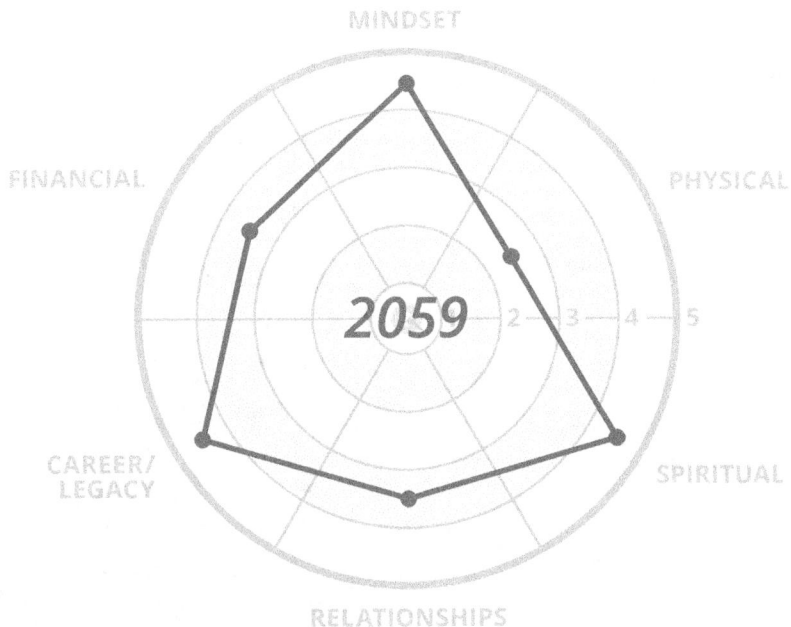

The plot points for most of the life facets look really good! Things are going great at work, really good at home and spiritually, okay financially and we're looking at a very good, positive mindset.

The 'flat' on this wheel is obvious. If we are not doing well in the physical arena, how might that affect our other life facets over time? Now take into consideration that the QTR year is prominently written in the center of the wheel. This should not only point out the areas in life that need work, attention and resources; it should add a sense of urgency. With only so much time (and we all start with the same 24 hours in a day), what will you spend yours on?

Before you do your Life Wheel, where do you think you'll come up flat? What is your gut telling you?

As you put pen to paper, be brutally honest with yourself. If you're doing this with a partner, I recommend you do it both for yourself and for each other.

You're going to want as much objectivity as possible to get the most out of the process.

Please do this exercise for 'My Current Life'; and rate yourself as of today.

Start by putting your QTR year at the center.

MY CURRENT LIFE

What does your wheel look like? Would it roll smoothly, or would you be bouncing along in a jarring, nerve wracking 'thump, thump, thump' that beats you up so bad you just want to pull over and stop the ride?

Hopefully this exercise brings your 'big picture' into focus. And rather than thinking of this as identifying your weaknesses, think of it as a quick way to highlight the areas you want to focus on and improve in the next 90 days.

The next exercise is easy. You're going to write your QTR year into the very center of the wheel, entitled 'My Preferred Life'. Then, rate yourself in each facet indicating your preferred future. SPOILER: If you don't plot all fives, you need to give this book to a friend!

MY PREFERRED LIFE

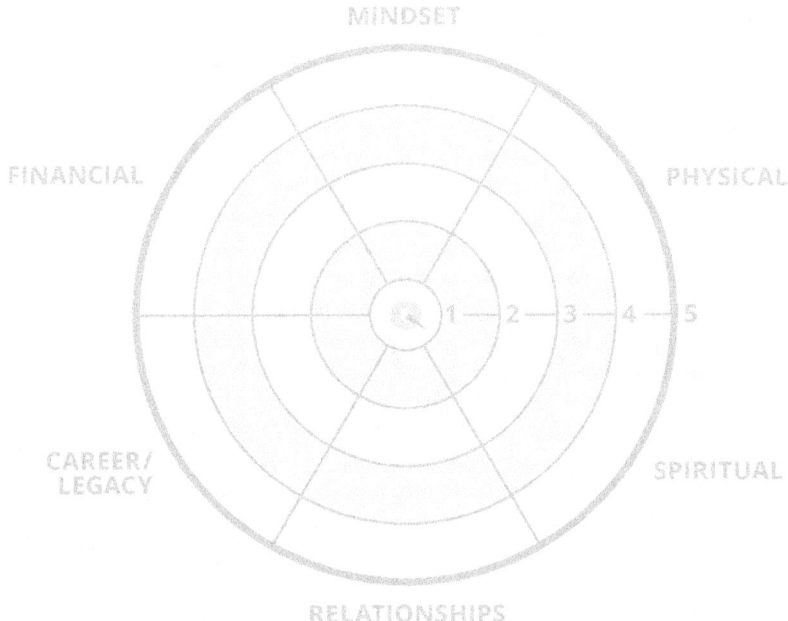

The point of the Life Wheel is to be able to quickly assess where you are in a snapshot. High level QTR practitioners will do this monthly, some even weekly. The best use it as a quick self-awareness assessment anytime they're feeling 'blocked'.

You'll need to find the rhythm that works best for you. Starting out, I'd recommend you revisit it at least quarterly, as a precursor to the QTR Challenges we'll cover next.

Pro Tip: More Facets Of Life

When you work with enough people on any given set of content, you'll start to notice the 'consumer mods' or modifications that arise. This is all a part of continuous improvement, and how great design can work.

The Life Wheel is one of the most common places mods happen. In the illustration below, someone has realized that 'Relationships' is a pretty big bucket, and they felt compelled to break it down further. There's the relationship with their significant other. Then the relationship with their children. Then parents on both sides; siblings...and what about friends?

Here's the Pro Tip: Simple Gets Done. It's your life, your wheel. Make it your own! But before you break it down into too many categories, reflect on what matters most and what you really want to work on in the time you have remaining. Remember, QTR starts with 'Quality'.

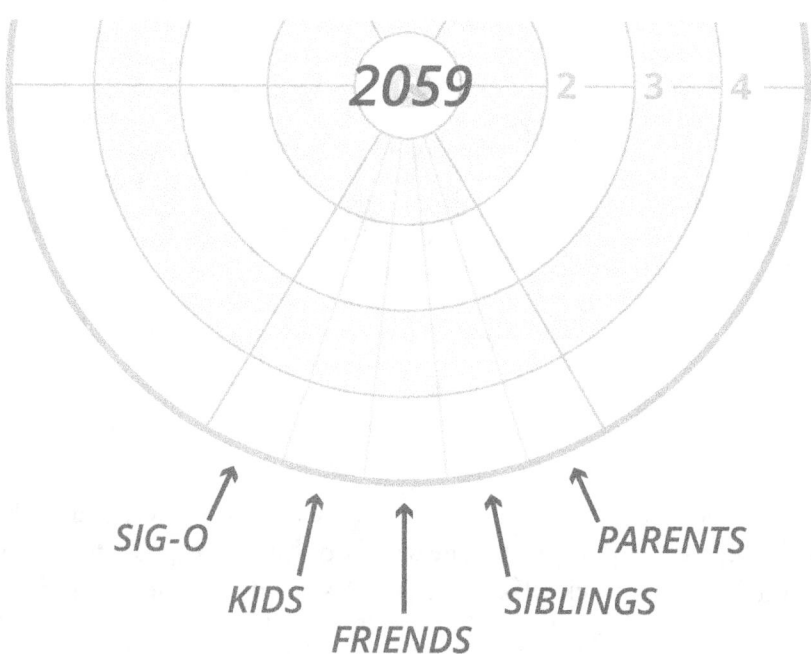

In the next illustration, you'll find an example that has kept me sane for years. I still want more 'facets' in relationships, but it's deliberately kept quite simple (Simple gets done). When I'm honest about priority, I know that focusing on my relationship with JoAnn is #1 in my life. And I chose 'Romance' as the facet name because it captures the spirit of how I want to approach that part of my life. It's probably an oversimplification to say, 'happy wife, happy life', but in the Ozarks we have a saying, "If Momma ain't happy, ain't nobody happy". If we're in a good place, I know that has a compounding effect on the rest of the family. Which leads us to 'Family of Creation'.

Mental health professionals look to our 'Family of Origin' to understand more about why we are who we are. This is the family in which we grew up. The one that shapes us at a very young age. It's widely accepted that most of our 'programming' happens by the time we are three to five years old. Whoa! No wonder we all struggle with some aspect of family life. The unwritten rules, the double standards, the self-blindness we often don't learn about until we have relationships outside the family.

I love the term 'Family of Creation'. This is the family we create for ourselves. The friends with which we surround ourselves. The support system we construct to get us through the tough times. The children we have. Who's in yours?

For me, I know my primary focus is on JoAnn, then the kids, then friends and family that make life so beautiful and fulfilling. Then there's room for the responsibilities of the Family of Origin, as long as there are strong boundaries to keep things healthy.

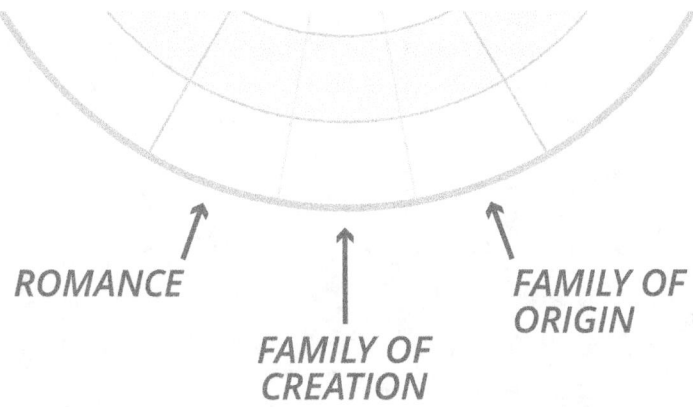

ROMANCE

FAMILY OF CREATION

FAMILY OF ORIGIN

Play with your Life Wheel. Do multiple versions until you feel it really reflects your life as it is, and your life as you want it to be. As you rate each facet (and any sub-facets you create), be sure to take into consideration the limited time you have. Use your QTR number and year as a source of power instead of fear. Remember, knowing how long the game will last can radically change the way we play it. This is the best way to give yourself permission to focus on what matters most in your life.

Next, we'll be using the QTR Challenges to help you dig deeper into each facet of your life.

06. THE QTR CHALLENGES

Almost Everything Will Work Again if you Unplug it for a Few Minutes, Including You.

Anne Lamott
b. 1954

06. THE QTR CHALLENGES

You need to unplug and invest some time in yourself if you expect to increase your Quality Time Remaining. The idea behind the QTR Challenges is to get you into the habit of reflecting frequently on the most important aspects of your life, one by one. The probing questions are designed to be approachable, but at the same time, challenging.

Using the Life Wheel exercise as an indicator of where you need to put your time, effort and resources, the Challenges will help you delve into any facet of your life in which you're struggling. For example, if Physical is rated a 2, and most of your other facets are 3, 4 and 5, do the QTR Challenge: Physical.

The Challenges are designed to be self-directed. It's wise to set aside 15-30 minutes of quiet time working through one of these Challenges. Some Practitioners report great success with doing one a week as part of their morning reflection practice. Others like to set aside a longer time slot, so they can do all the Challenges and look at the global view of their Quality Time Remaining. Personally, I go through all 6 challenges as part of my quarterly planning.

Each Challenge will ask you to reflect on these questions:

What can you celebrate?
How are you growing?
How are you decaying?
How can you blunt decay?
How can you ignite growth?
What are you fighting for?

What's one action you can take to increase your happiness?
What action can you truly commit to accomplishing?
How will it feel to accomplish it?
What will it cost you if you don't?
When will you celebrate?

The QTR Challenges are important to the rhythm and accountability of the entire system. If you have a coach or accountability group, include QTR in your weekly discussions. If you don't have that option, put it on your calendar now, and keep up the rhythm. Aside from 'doing the work' itself, the real secret to QTR is twofold: discipline and frequency. Your engagement and motivation will be significantly better the more often you practice, and your results will be nothing short of remarkable.

Conversely, like everything else in life, let it slide and you'll see your engagement, motivation, and results (AND your Quality Time Remaining) slide along with it.

As you embark on these Challenges, I'll give you some advice once given me by Dr. Mike Zwell. He said, "Be Selfish". That's a pretty tall order for a natural people pleaser and chronic 'fixer' like me. In other words, QTR is for *you*. The more you put into the process, the more you'll get out of it. So, give yourself permission to spend time and effort on you. You can't care for others if you have nothing to give.

At the end of each Challenge, there are also suggestions for inspirational reading. Keep in mind, these reading lists are not exhaustive, nor are they required. But they do include some timeless wisdom and hopefully, some things some things that are new to you.

One more thing. As you immerse yourself in the work, be aware of your programming and your limiting beliefs. Author Brianna Wiest says it beautifully:

> *"Limiting beliefs are when you negotiate yourself into a smaller goal. This is why you need to go beyond your current view of yourself."*
> *Brianna Wiest*
> *b. 1992*

We are not very good predictors of our future selves. Try and picture not only what you want now, but what you will want as a growing, changing, evolving person. You'll be glad you went the extra mile.

07. QTR CHALLENGE: MINDSET

Truckers Don't Have 'Trucker's Block'. They Get Up and Drive.

Steven Pressfield
b. 1943

07. QTR CHALLENGE: MINDSET

Our mindset consists of the beliefs that inform how we look at the world. Gandhi is quoted as saying, "Your beliefs become your thoughts. Your thoughts become your words. Your words become your actions. Your actions become your habits. Your habits become your values. Your values become your destiny."

It's a simple interpolation to go from this:

Beliefs → Thoughts → Words → Actions → Habits → Values → Destiny

To this:

Beliefs → Destiny

Consider the phrase, 'Your mindset becomes your destiny'. You've likely known someone with a fixed mindset, and they don't stray too far from the farm, so to speak. You wouldn't be reading QTR if you didn't feel a strong desire to go after what you want, so it's probably safe to assume you're working with a growth mindset. Whether you have a fixed or growth mindset, your beliefs will indeed become your destiny.

If you've studied the power of a growth mindset, you've probably run across Dr. Carol Dweck, author of *Mindset-The New Psychology of Success*. This is a must-read for a growth-oriented person.

Dr. Dweck states that "The hallmark of successful people is that they are always stretching themselves to learn new things. When there's a setback, someone with a fixed mindset will start thinking, 'Maybe I don't have what it takes? ' They may get defensive and give up. A hallmark of a successful person is that they persist in the face of obstacle, and often, these obstacles are blessings in disguise."

If you aren't scrutinizing your Mindset on a frequent basis, it's incredibly easy to backslide into a fixed mindset, which can inhibit not only your growth, but also your motivation.

A fixed mindset is stuck in the past, tethering you to a limiting belief system that can affect every facet of your life. It's easier to recognize a fixed mindset in someone else. "No, I don't want to do that, I'm just not that smart/athletic/ rich/capable" or "I'm too old to learn a new language/skill/way of doing things".

Henry Ford said, "Whether you think you can, or think you can't, you're right." A long time before Henry Ford, in a galaxy far, far away, Luke Skywalker whines, "I don't believe it!" Yoda replies, "That is why you fail."

A fixed mindset creeps in quietly, gradually, when you're not looking. The best way to combat it is to commit to lifelong learning and continuous improvement. Embrace the sense of wonder and curiosity you had when you were a child. Keep in mind that the QTR process is meant to be enlightening, challenging and fun, like most good things in life.

> *"Live as if you were to die tomorrow;*
> *learn as if you were to live forever."*
> *Mahatma Gandhi*
> *1869-1948*

Each of the Challenges is designed to stand alone, so you can always go back to any facet in your Life Wheel when you have a 'flat'. You can jump around and do them in any order you please. My suggestion is to complete them all, so you can get a global picture of what you'd like to accomplish in your life.

Preceding each of the Challenge Exercises, you'll find an example designed to give you guidance and inspiration. But don't lean on them too much. The quality of your outcomes depends entirely on the quality of your input. Give these challenges some serious thought; you'll be pleased and often surprised with your results.

Your answers may be more detailed and require more writing space. Go for it! Make it yours. Now, set aside some quiet time alone, work hard and good luck!

QTR CHALLENGE: MINDSET

EXAMPLE

Celebrate: What is Something You can be Proud of or Grateful for?

Recording a new podcast episode was engaging and fun this week. It should also drive engagement to my website.

What is One Way You Have Grown Your Mindset This Week?

Doing the prep, the research and the reading has been challenging but also gratifying. The interviews are so much better, too.

What is One Way You Have Allowed Mindset Decay This Week?

Procrastination! Why do I hit a wall sometimes? Why am I binging this Netflix series instead of reading??

List One Strategy You Can Use to Identify & Blunt Decay this Week:

Create a timeline and list for the latest project. Use streaming only as a reward when successfully completed.

List One Strategy You Can Use to Ignite Growth:

Start early in the day and be consistent with that. I am fresher, more creative and motivated in the morning. Use the afternoon for more mundane tasks.

Are You Fighting for What You Really Want?

Yes!! My goals are clear. I need to continue to draw line of sight from my daily actions and decisions to my larger goals.

List One Action You Can Take, Increasing Your Internal Control & Happiness:

I am far happier when I'm creating than when I'm consuming.

Which Strategy/Action Can You Truly Commit to Accomplishing This Week?

I also know that I'm more creative when I'm well rested. My one action is plan my day the night before, and to get a good night's sleep.

Visualize: How Will it Feel to Accomplish it?

From experience, I know it's the right thing to do, and I do in fact feel and perform better. Plus, I'll feel better about setting that small goal and achieving it.

Visualize: What Will it Cost You if You Don't?

Running on empty is not as easy as it was when I was younger. I need to remember the recovery time is much longer now, and time is not a commodity I want to spend irresponsibly.

Set a Date to Celebrate:

September 26th

QTR CHALLENGE: MINDSET

WORKSHEET

Celebrate: What is Something You can be Proud of or Grateful for?

What is One Way You Have Grown Your Mindset This Week?

What is One Way You Have Allowed Mindset Decay This Week?

List One Strategy You Can Use to Identify & Blunt Decay this Week:

List One Strategy You Can Use to Ignite Growth:

Are You Fighting for What You Really Want?

List One Action You Can Take, Increasing Your Internal Control & Happiness:

Which Strategy/Action Can You Truly Commit to Accomplishing This Week?

Visualize: How Will it Feel to Accomplish it?

Visualize: What Will it Cost You if You Don't?

Set a Date to Celebrate:

READING FOR INSPIRATION:

Mindset – The New Psychology of Success
by Carol Dweck

Man's Search for Meaning
by Viktor Frankl

The Big Leap
by Gay Hendricks

A Framework for Understanding Poverty
by Ruby Payne

Think and Grow Rich
by Napoleon Hill

As a Man Thinketh
by James Allen

The Magic of Thinking Big
by David Schwartz

See You at the Top
by Zig Ziglar

08. QTR CHALLENGE: PHYSICAL

How Young Can You be to Die of Old Age?

Steven Wright
b. 1955

08. QTR CHALLENGE: PHYSICAL

The next facet of life you should look at is Physical. Surely someone in your life has told you, "If you don't have your health, you don't have anything." Timeless wisdom. I hope you don't have to have a medical 'event' that spurs you to action, because it's much easier to start and maintain changes in your physical lifestyle when you're feeling good. But let's face it. For most of us, a kick in the pants is sometimes what we need.

Several years ago, I was coaching a cargo airline in the Southeast. It was a real eye-opener for me, because as a lifelong airline passenger, I was honestly a bit jaded to the experience of flying. These guys owned about a dozen MD-11's and 747's. Except not regular planes; these were cargo planes. They were completely empty except for an elaborate roller system built into the floor.

A Boeing 747-8 freighter has a maximum takeoff weight of 975,000 pounds. Imagine it. This is like throwing a million pounds into the air and having it stick! This feat shouldn't be possible at all, yet this airline was doing it every day. They carried everything you can imagine – food, flowers, military hardware, even pallet loads of currency. One of the pilots showed me photos of live camels being moved via air freight!

While in Miami at Boeing's training center, they snuck me into a flight simulator so I could experience what it was like to fly one of these behemoths. That's when I first learned that these aircraft were far from new. In fact, most were between 40 and 50 years old. About the time I picked my jaw up from the floor, the maintenance manager taught me that they really weren't half a century old. You see, these aircraft are on an FAA calendaric maintenance schedule. Whether they fly the plane of not, parts are replaced on a time-constrained basis. Fly it more, and that schedule accelerates.

Your body is not dissimilar. Dr. Henry Lodge, author of *Younger Next Year*, states that "70% of aging is not real aging. It's rot from the stuff we do."

Can you believe that nearly three quarters of age-related disease is reversible? If you sit on the couch eating nachos all the time, your muscles will atrophy, and your body composition will dramatically change (along with your health). If you stress your body with exercise, it will maintain and even grow new muscle and bone. A healthy, exercised thigh muscle will replace itself, cell by cell, every 3 to 4 months. Your stomach lining replaces itself every few days. That's amazing! Unfortunately, your brain cells don't do that (which they could have told me in the 80's.)

It's called catabolism. Your body transmits signals to your brain that a muscle is not being used. Then your brain sends out the wrecking crew to begin tearing down that muscle, molecule by molecule. The opposite is anabolism (think anabolic steroids). Stress that muscle and it will repair and grow.

> ## "We must all either wear out or rust out— every one of us. My choice is to wear out."
> ### Theodore Roosevelt
> ### 1858-1919

The cargo airline helped me see that I'd much rather be that big, beautiful 747 in the sky doing impossible things – rather than the burned-out old shell of a plane they retired to the Mojave Desert Boneyard for spare parts.

As someone with a lot of life experience, I've benefited from the lessons of time. When I was young and bulletproof, I took risks and had adventures I honestly would not even consider today. And with age, things hurt. If you're in your twenties and thirties, I challenge you to spend time with someone older than you that you respect and trust. Ask them what they did right, and what they'd do differently. Then suspend your disbelief and make one small change in your physical approach to life. Your future self will thank you.

If you are more, umm, 'mature' (I've never been accused of being mature), think back to what we discussed around limiting beliefs and fixed mindset. It doesn't matter what adventures you're considering, there's probably a 90-year-old some-where in the world doing it right now. Anything's possible. As with everything in QTR, what do you really want?

QTR CHALLENGE: PHYSICAL

EXAMPLE

Celebrate: What is Something You can be Proud of or Grateful for?

Cut my sugar intake in half. Wasn't that bad. Lowered my glucose levels by 5 points!

What is One Way You Have Grown Physically This Week?

Doing better on nutrition; making better choices and eliminating sugary snacks at the house and work.

What is One Way You Have Allowed Physical Decay This Week?

Still not getting enough sleep, which makes me tired and not want to workout.

List One Strategy You Can Use to Identify & Blunt Decay this Week:

Set my 'bedtime' to 10:30PM, and put an alarm on it! Get into a routine.

List One Strategy You Can Use to Ignite Growth:

Set a reasonable wake time, and be consistent. 6:00AM is doable. 5:00AM is stupid.

Are You Fighting for What You Really Want?

Yes. Seeing my blood sugar is in my control really motivates me, and I don't want to let disease take me away from what I love most.

List One Action You Can Take, Increasing Your Internal Control & Happiness:

Come to grips with the fact that I am my own worst enemy or greatest advocate.

Which Strategy/Action Can You Truly Commit to Accomplishing This Week?

Setting the alarms for 'bedtime' and 'wake time'... and sticking to them for one week.

Visualize: How Will it Feel to Accomplish it?

I already feel I'm making progress, and feeling less guilt. I can't wait to see how freeing this will feel!

Visualize: What Will it Cost You if You Don't?

My health, my energy, my appearance, my confidence, my peace of mind... the list goes on.

Set a Date to Celebrate:

October 15.

QTR CHALLENGE: PHYSICAL

WORKSHEET

Celebrate: What is Something You can be Proud of or Grateful for?

What is One Way You Have Grown Physically This Week?

What is One Way You Have Allowed Physical Decay This Week?

List One Strategy You Can Use to Identify & Blunt Decay this Week:

List One Strategy You Can Use to Ignite Growth:

Are You Fighting for What You Really Want?

List One Action You Can Take, Increasing Your Internal Control & Happiness:

Which Strategy/Action Can You Truly Commit to Accomplishing This Week?

Visualize: How Will it Feel to Accomplish it?

Visualize: What Will it Cost You if You Don't?

Set a Date to Celebrate:

READING FOR INSPIRATION:

Note: There will always be an ever growing list of popular titles on the subject.

Titles include *Outlive*, *Lifespan*, *How Not to Age*, *How Not to Die*, etc.

Keep reading, keep learning, and keep a healthy skepticism as you go. Stick to simple, timeless wisdom rather than what's on the best seller list.

Here are a few favorites:

Younger Next Year
by Chris Crowley & Henry S. Lodge

The Blue Zones
by Dan Buettner

Darebee.com
or any good bodyweight resistance program.

09. QTR CHALLENGE: FINANCIAL

The Ability to do What You Want, When You Want, With Who You Want, For as Long as You Want, Pays The Highest Dividend That Exists in Finance.

Morgan Housel
b. 1990

09. QTR CHALLENGE: FINANCIAL

Now you're getting the hang of this. The Financial Challenge will probably bring a lot of your old programming to the surface. Were you raised in a household where money was never talked about, or was money a hot topic that was always being 'discussed' in colorful terms?

In the United States, chances are no matter what you learned about money as a kid is just plain wrong. Bankrate's research states the 82% of Americans are significantly stressed about their financial situation. A recent study by Experian® shows 59% of divorcees say that money issues played a big role in their divorces.

I've been writing, speaking, and coaching on open-book management for nearly 20 years, and can tell you that most entrepreneurs are really not all that comfortable with their own financials. The United States is simply not a nation of financially literate people. One reason is that we spend $670,000,000 on financial education in this country, while financial services companies spend $17,000,000,000 on marketing financial products (think 'credit'). You read that right. 670 *million* against 17 *billion*. So, for every U.S. citizen, that's about $2 in education against $50 in marketing. It's not a fair fight.

The bottom line is this: You're okay. You're not dumb, you're not bad, you're not crazy. You are just...normal. Wherever you are now, get better. Use the Financial Challenge to take small steps to improve your situation.

And if you happen to be in great financial shape, use the Challenge to take yourself to the next level.

All you want to do is figure out for yourself where you're winning, where you're losing, and what you're not admitting to yourself. Restructure your relationship with money.

Whatever you find, you're right. Counselors use the phrase, "Name it to tame it." Name something you want to change about how you relate to money, and you'll immediately start taking control of your financial life. And as we learned before, that even a little bit of control helps increase our happiness. Your action steps might include reading a book, attending a class or taking an online course.

For those of you doing QTR with a partner, find time to explore both of your histories and unwritten rules about money. You'll want to find as much common ground as possible, realizing the best way forward lies somewhere between the two of your perspectives. I remember the expression of sheer joy on JoAnn's face the day we read that I was the 'nerd' and she was the 'free spirit budget adjuster'".

Have you ever found yourself wondering how you got into a financial bind? It doesn't matter if you took a payday loan out of panic or lost a ton of money on an over-hyped stock or cryptocurrency. Hindsight may be 20/20, but why do we often find ourselves in a not too different bind later in life as well?

Because we didn't change our relationship with money. The German philosopher Georg Hegel said, "The only thing we learn from history is that we learn nothing from history." Our programming, habits, and patterns will repeat themselves until we face them and change them for the better.

So, I want you to challenge yourself, but, I also want you to be kind. Morgan Housel says, "Some people are born into families that encourage education; others are against it. Some are born into flourishing economies encouraging of entrepreneurship; others are born into war and destitution. I want you to be successful, and I want you to earn it. But realize that not all success is due to hard work, and not all poverty is due to laziness. Keep this in mind when judging people, including yourself."

And finally, don't try to be too smart. Warren Buffet's long time partner at Berkshire-Hathaway captures this sentiment perfectly.

> *"It's remarkable how much long-term advantage people like us have gotten by trying to be consistently not stupid, instead of trying to be very intelligent."*
> *Charlie Munger*
> *1924-2023*

My goal is to be more like Charlie Munger and be 'consistently not stupid'. Use the QTR Financial Challenge to help you do the same.

QTR CHALLENGE: FINANCIAL

EXAMPLE

Celebrate: What is Something You can be Proud of or Grateful for?

Just created a budget together. Already feeling more aligned and in control.

What is One Way You Have Grown Financially This Week?

The budget was a big step forward; we are joining a personal finance class provided by work.

What is One Way You Have Allowed Financial Decay This Week?

Actually looking at how much money we spend on eating at restaurants is almost obscene! But we don't have that spending under any control yet.

List One Strategy You Can Use to Identify & Blunt Decay this Week:

Paying in cash will be a big help. 'Feeling the transaction' will make an impact.

List One Strategy You Can Use to Ignite Growth:

Creating the budget is one thing. Meeting weekly will make a huge difference. But learning is going to be integral to our success. The class and reading will help.

Are You Fighting for What You Really Want?

We are now. Feeling so out of control for so long has been a subconscious drag on everything. Fighting for financial independence is vital to our big picture.

List One Action You Can Take, Increasing Your Internal Control & Happiness:

Living on a budget already feels 'do-able'. I feel more in control.

Which Strategy/Action Can You Truly Commit to Accomplishing This Week?

My one action is plan the week's spending, and carry cash for any expenses.

Visualize: How Will it Feel to Accomplish it?

It will feel amazing to not be in survival mode or sheer ignorance! I can already feel a lift.

Visualize: What Will it Cost You if You Don't?

I never want to feel 'behind' again. If we don't do this, we'll always be indentured to an uncaring machine.

Set a Date to Celebrate:

June 1st

QTR CHALLENGE: FINANCIAL

WORKSHEET

Celebrate: What is Something You can be Proud of or Grateful for?

What is One Way You Have Grown Financially This Week?

What is One Way You Have Allowed Financial Decay This Week?

List One Strategy You Can Use to Identify & Blunt Decay this Week:

List One Strategy You Can Use to Ignite Growth:

Are You Fighting for What You Really Want?

List One Action You Can Take, Increasing Your Internal Control & Happiness:

Which Strategy/Action Can You Truly Commit to Accomplishing This Week?

Visualize: How Will it Feel to Accomplish it?

Visualize: What Will it Cost You if You Don't?

Set a Date to Celebrate:

READING FOR INSPIRATION:

The Psychology of Money
by Morgan Housel

Prosperity in the Age of Decline
by Alan & Brian Beaulieu

The Millionaire Next Door: The Surprising Secrets of America's Wealthy
by Thomas J. Stanley and William D. Danko

The Psychology of Human Misjudgment
by Charlie Munger

The Complete Guide to Money
by Dave Ramsey

The Richest Man in Babylon
by George S. Clason

Die with Zero
by Bill Perkins

10. QTR CHALLENGE: RELATIONSHIPS

In Life, You Get What You Tolerate.

Dr. Henry Cloud
b. 1956

10. QTR CHALLENGE: RELATIONSHIPS

Quality Time Remaining sounds like the title of a relationship book, doesn't it? Why wait until now to talk about them? It is my belief that you can't be in the best frame of mind to work on a relationship with someone else until you are in the best frame of mind with yourself.

American psychologist Abraham Maslow's "Hierarchy of Needs" theorized that five basic needs dictate people's behavior from survival to ultimate self-actualization. At the base of his hierarchy are physiological needs like breathing, eating, sleeping. Then comes security; am I safe here? Will I have a job, do I have enough money and resources to live? Only then can we get into belonging and relationships.

By first reflecting on our own mindset, our physical well-being, and our financial security, we are better equipped to look at our relationships more clearly. And that's how we'll get the best outcomes.

Rather than pose as some relationship guru, let me just say that I am quite the opposite. I am not a relationship expert, nor do I pretend to be. I am a student, and probably a C student at best. But that gives me a superpower. Being self-aware of that fact has made me a lifelong learner. And QTR is not about being an expert on all things, it's about creating the life you truly want, when you strip away all of the ancillary stuff with which we unconsciously surround ourselves.

My desire to understand more about how to relate to other people, especially people I love, has driven me to consume an inordinate amount of material on the subject through the years. Since you are reading this, I'd bet you're in my class.

I love the phrase, "Your life is perfectly designed for the results you're currently getting." This riff on W. Edwards Deming's timeless wisdom is so simple, yet so powerful, you can find it on dozens of life coach websites, unattributed. If you really take it in, and you're honest with yourself, it might just shock your system enough to change your life.

What is your life perfectly designed for?

Doctors Judith and Bob Wright's book *Heart of the Fight* describes the 'Rules of Engagement' in relationships. My favorite states that we are all 100% responsible for our own happiness and satisfaction, and no one is responsible for more than 50% of the blame. Whether you agree or disagree, consider this. Have you ever found yourself relegating your happiness to another person, or attributing most of the blame in a situation to someone else? It's human nature. We have to transcend our nature and learn how to be better, if we want extraordinary, lasting relationships.

What are you doing to grow? Consuming books, blogs, and videos are a great start. In our society, the stigma of seeking help seems to be slowly lifting. Still, you know the statistics. Half of relationships end in a split. What are you willing to invest in order to improve or even save your most precious relationships? It may cost you time, effort, and money...but are you willing to look at your own pride and ignorance?

> *"Successful relationships start by giving up control, giving up the need to be loved or wanted or right all the time."*
> *Mark Manson*
> *b. 1984*

I urge you to use the QTR Relationship Challenge to take a hard look at yourself and your approach to your relationships. It's worth quoting Brianna Wiest again. "Things get better with time, not because time heals, but because you grow. Life didn't get easier, you got smarter." So get smarter! Life will indeed get better.

Keep in mind that most people today have a tendency to leave well enough alone. 'If it ain't broke, don't fix it' is not a winning strategy here. Your relationships will grow, with or without you. The question is, are you growing together or apart?

This Challenge is designed to help you get objective about the most important relationships in your life, often the same ones we tend to neglect, overlook or put off. Use this opportunity to ask yourself, "Am I happy with the way my relationships are going? What do I really want? Where is this headed?"

Then it's your job to take one action that will make the biggest impact on your happiness and long-term, sustainable life satisfaction. Give this exercise the time it deserves.

QTR CHALLENGE: RELATIONSHIPS

EXAMPLE

Celebrate: What is Something You can be Proud of or Grateful for?

What a phenomenal holiday we had! Everyone was there, very little drama. Put this one in the 'win' column!

What is One Way You Have Grown Your Relationships This Week?

Spending downtime with the TV off has been very good for us. Need to do that more.

What is One Way You Have Allowed a Relationship to Decay This Week?

I have really been lax in contacting old friends; really lax. I can't wait on someone else to make the first call. I have got to do it myself.

List One Strategy You Can Use to Identify & Blunt Decay this Week:

Got to make a list of the folks that mean the most to me, and get those calls on the calendar. There's just no other way for me.

List One Strategy You Can Use to Ignite Growth:

The calendar is one, but I also want to work on my active listening skills, too.

Are You Fighting for What You Really Want?

After so many years of trying to please other people, this is imperative to my own mental and emotional health, and for that of my Family of Creation.

List One Action You Can Take, Increasing Your Internal Control & Happiness:

In one word: reconnection.

Which Strategy/Action Can You Truly Commit to Accomplishing This Week?

My next action is to make the list of people and make the first 3 calls.

Visualize: How Will it Feel to Accomplish it?

Historically, I always feel a charge after talking with old, dear friends, so why don't I do it more?

Visualize: What Will it Cost You if You Don't?

Isolation is a bad echo chamber. Relationships are at the very core of why we live vs. survive. I choose to live.

Set a Date to Celebrate:

November 11th

QTR CHALLENGE: RELATIONSHIPS

WORKSHEET

Celebrate: What is Something You can be Proud of or Grateful for?

What is One Way You Have Grown Your Relationships This Week?

What is One Way You Have Allowed a Relationship to Decay This Week?

List One Strategy You Can Use to Identify & Blunt Decay this Week:

List One Strategy You Can Use to Ignite Growth:

Are You Fighting for What You Really Want?

List One Action You Can Take, Increasing Your Internal Control & Happiness:

Which Strategy/Action Can You Truly Commit to Accomplishing This Week?

Visualize: How Will it Feel to Accomplish it?

Visualize: What Will it Cost You if You Don't?

Set a Date to Celebrate:

READING FOR INSPIRATION:

The Road Less Traveled
by M. Scott Peck

Boundaries
by Henry Cloud

The Five Love Languages
by Gary Chapman

The Four Agreements
by Don Miguel Ruiz

The Power of TED: The Empowerment Dynamic
by David Emerald

Be sure to explore:
- **John Gottman**
- **Stephen Karpman**
- **Brene Brown**
- **John Gray**
- **Elizabeth Kubler-Ross**

11. QTR CHALLENGE: SPIRITUAL

God is a Comedian Playing to an Audience Too Afraid to Laugh.

Voltaire
1694–1778

11. QTR CHALLENGE: SPIRITUAL

Through the years, I've gotten so much flack for the Voltaire quote, you'd think I'd use something else to introduce the Spiritual facet of life. There is so much about religion that gets us wound up around the axle, I think many people lose sight of what I'm really trying to get at. I'm not talking about religion. I'm talking about your individual relationship with the divine, a higher power, God. I'm talking about your faith; what you truly believe in. Let's focus on a connection that is sacred and personal to you.

Last year, I taught a 9-week course on QTR, with people from numerous backgrounds and belief systems. I shared a photo of a time we had the opportunity to see Pope John Paul II in St. Louis with a quarter of a million other people. When the Pope-mobile entered the TWA Dome, the entire stadium fell utterly silent. So still was the crowd, that even from the 3rd tier up, we could hear the Mercedes idling. The sheer *reverence* of the crowd is what moved us so deeply.

But that's not how everyone saw it. You'd think I'd just kicked their dog. Some immediately focused on the Pope, Catholicism, religion, dogma, rather than the experience I was trying to convey. I'm pretty sure that I would've gotten the same response if the story would've been about the Dali Lama or Billy Graham. Religion can be terribly polarizing.

It's safe to say we all know a few agnostics. Through the years, I have met more than a few atheists. At one point, a client got me access to the Hubbard School of Business in Los Angeles (Yup. The Scientologists.) I've seen so many diverse approaches to faith, it's mind-boggling. Admittedly, I've only been exposed to a tiny fraction of the world's 10,000 documented religions. It's downright humbling. Everyone is on their own journey. That, I can respect. No matter what your inclination, take this Challenge seriously.

Your own spiritual history is something you'll need to come to grips with, regardless of whether it was positive or negative. What works for you? What doesn't work for you? How does your spirituality interplay with your relationships? What do you expect from it?

Have you studied, I mean *really* studied, your faith? Have you ever studied a faith outside your own? It's not about abandoning your beliefs. Rather, it's about exposing yourself to the similarities and wild differences you'll find. Maybe you'll come to appreciate nature more by reading about the Shinto faith. Maybe you'll be more tolerant by learning about Islam or Judaism. Or maybe you'll gain an objectivity about Christianity that allows you to see how much we all have in common. And who doesn't love the timeless wisdom of the ancient Greeks, the Tao, Confucius, and Buddha?

In *The Rhythm of Life*, Matthew Kelly says, "Love is the central precept and principle to every major religion. It is the answer to every question. It is the solution to every problem. The answer is never to love less, the answer is always to love more."

However the Spiritual Challenge may open your mind, my intent is to have you thinking bigger than yourself.

What does spirituality mean to you? Is it feeling connected to a higher power, or a sense of belonging in the universe? Is it the search for purpose and meaning? What practices help you get outside yourself? Is it walking in nature? Is it meditation? Maybe for you it's a spending time in an ancient cathedral. Whatever it is, do it. For this challenge put yourself in the environment that works.

> *"It's ironic that in our culture everyone's biggest complaint is about not having enough time; yet nothing terrifies us more than the thought of eternity."*
> *Dennis Miller*
> *b. 1953*

The Spiritual Challenge may be more difficult than you think. Try to not let dogmatic interference hinder you from the task at hand. Keep clutter and noise to a minimum. Your assignment here is to get in touch with what you truly want and need out of your spiritual life, what's in the way, and what you're willing to do to improve it.

QTR CHALLENGE: SPIRITUAL

EXAMPLE

Celebrate: What is Something You can be Proud of or Grateful for?

I'm quite proud of how I helped a colleague think through a tough situation this week. Just 'holding space' for them did wonders for them, and for me.

What is One Way You Have Grown Spiritually This Week?

The feeling I got from that interaction has shown me that helping others in this way is tremendously rewarding for me too.

What is One Way You Have Allowed Spiritual Decay This Week?

Intellectually I know that holding on to old hurts is only hurting me, but forgiveness is so hard! I need help getting better at that.

List One Strategy You Can Use to Identify & Blunt Decay this Week:

If I can document complaint, resentment, and other negative thoughts, I can start to get them under control. Maybe I can make a quick note in my phone.

List One Strategy You Can Use to Ignite Growth:

If I do grab quick notes on my phone, growth will come from reviewing them. I can add that to my weekly review process.

Are You Fighting for What You Really Want?

This ties in so well with my relationships and to my ultimate goal of freedom.

List One Action You Can Take, Increasing Your Internal Control & Happiness:

Identify one person I need to forgive, and work to set myself free.

Which Strategy/Action Can You Truly Commit to Accomplishing This Week?

This week, I will use my phone's auto-dictate task list to quickly document negative thoughts and review them at the end of the week.

Visualize: How Will it Feel to Accomplish it?

This should help me identify opportunities for forgiveness, as well as patterns and old limiting beliefs about people and situations. That will feel pretty good.

Visualize: What Will it Cost You if You Don't?

I met a much older person recently who was still talking about something that happened to them in high school. I refuse to be held hostage by things in the past that just don't matter!

Set a Date to Celebrate:

August 7th.

QTR CHALLENGE: SPIRITUAL

WORKSHEET

Celebrate: What is Something You can be Proud of or Grateful for?

What is One Way You Have Grown Spiritually This Week?

What is One Way You Have Allowed Spiritual Decay This Week?

List One Strategy You Can Use to Identify & Blunt Decay this Week:

List One Strategy You Can Use to Ignite Growth:

Are You Fighting for What You Really Want?

List One Action You Can Take, Increasing Your Internal Control & Happiness:

Which Strategy/Action Can You Truly Commit to Accomplishing This Week?

Visualize: How Will it Feel to Accomplish it?

Visualize: What Will it Cost You if You Don't?

Set a Date to Celebrate:

READING FOR INSPIRATION:

At the time of this writing 84% of the world's population identifies with a religious group. The five major religions are Christianity, Islam, Buddhism, Hinduism, and Judaism.

Rather than a recommended reading list, I'll make a different suggestion. Why not study more deeply the faith you identify with? Then, consider studying another belief system outside your own?

That's a growth mindset.

12. QTR CHALLENGE: CAREER/LEGACY

The Idea is Not to Live Forever, but to Create Something That Will.

Andy Warhol
1928–1987

Let's talk about work. The average American spends far more time at work than they do with the people they love. Wait. That sounded like we all hate our co-workers. Let's look at the numbers.

You'll remember that I started the book with these stats from the Bureau of Labor Statistics:

The average person will spend thirty percent of their life sleeping, thirty percent going to school and working, twenty percent eating, shopping, child-rearing, commuting. Twelve percent will be flushed on TV, video games and social media. What's left? Eight percent? Roughly 6 years left to...live.

Shocking as it may seem, we do let an awful lot of our lives slip through the cracks. And work for you is probably not average...not just 40 hours a week. So, let's get serious. Is your work meaningful, engaging and fulfilling?

Remember, QTR is not about doomsday, it's about freedom. It's about giving yourself permission to focus on the things and people that make life worth living. Take this time to get realigned with your other goals, your other facets, and leverage your professional life to enhance everything else you want.

The Bureau of Labor Statistics it's estimates that there are two jobs for every person in the workforce. Their data indicates this trend is not going away any time soon. Use this to your advantage; find work that will impact the other facets of your life in a positive way.

There is one axiom that I believe with all my being. You make your own luck. If there's one thing I can impart to younger readers, don't wait for something to happen. Put yourself in the position of best opportunity. Find a mentor. Be an intern. Volunteer if there's something you're passionate about.

Despite her many flaws, America is still the best place in our universe to go after what you want, and actually have a shot at getting it. Still, this doesn't happen over night for most of us. You've got work and keep working. The man who taught me business, Jack Stack, says that the difference between amateurs and champions, is that champions have learned to train through the boredom.

> *"Everything comes to him who*
> *hustles while he waits."*
> *Thomas Edison*
> *1847-1941*

One wish I have for you and anyone you love: Never, never, take on work for survival if you can help it. I hope you are able to choose, so that you can keep as much internal control over your life as possible. That internal locus of control, as we discussed earlier, is vital to your long-term happiness and sustainable satisfaction.

For those of you on the other end of the timeline, the Career/Legacy Challenge should help you sort out what mark you want to leave. What dent do you want to make in the universe?

It's still hard for me to believe many of the people I came up with now lead corporations and not-for-profits. For many, one's legacy may not be obvious. If that's you, go beyond thinking about the job, the goals, the short-term plans. How have you changed your industry? How have you impacted the lives of your co-workers? What have you helped to create? How have you made the world just a tiny bit better?

You've heard the old saying, "on your deathbed, you'll never say you wished you'd spent more time at work." So, what would you want your epitaph to say? What if you lived what some would call a 'eulogy-centered life'. Time for you to get into the exercise.

QTR CHALLENGE: CAREER/LEGACY

EXAMPLE

Celebrate: What is Something You can be Proud of or Grateful for?

Enrolling in Continuing Education was the right move. I've got to make time to expand my understanding and knowledge to remain relevant.

What is One Way You Have Grown in Your Career/Legacy This Week?

Starting to mentor potential successors has been enlightening. I'm starting to understand the old aphorism, "a rising tide lifts all ships".

What is One Way You Have Allowed Decay This Week?

Resting on my laurels. It's been a good year, work-wise, but I cannot allow myself to become complacent in such a dynamic marketplace.

List One Strategy You Can Use to Identify & Blunt Decay this Week:

Continuing Ed is one way; I probably need to look for decay more than expecting to have it just appear. Decay is more insidious than that.

List One Strategy You Can Use to Ignite Growth:

Budget for 30 minutes a day for reading and learning on a work related topic.

Are You Fighting for What You Really Want?

Yes. Everyone wants meaningful work; helping others find theirs seems to be a big part of what I want to do.

List One Action You Can Take, Increasing Your Internal Control & Happiness:

I am definitely more fulfilled the more I learn and the more I share with someone ready to receive it.

Which Strategy/Action Can You Truly Commit to Accomplishing This Week?

Going back to the calendar, I will need to time-block each week so minutia doesn't erode the time I could be spending on learning/growing/mentoring.

Visualize: How Will it Feel to Accomplish it?

The fulfillment, the satisfaction, the pride of it all will feel empowering.

Visualize: What Will it Cost You if You Don't?

Time is a finite quantity. Am I really going to deny myself and others of the opportunity to grow? The cost would be enormous.

Set a Date to Celebrate:

March 30th

QTR CHALLENGE: CAREER/LEGACY

WORKSHEET

Celebrate: What is Something You can be Proud of or Grateful for?

What is One Way You Have Grown in Your Career/Legacy This Week?

What is One Way You Have Allowed Decay This Week?

List One Strategy You Can Use to Identify & Blunt Decay this Week:

List One Strategy You Can Use to Ignite Growth:

Are You Fighting for What You Really Want?

List One Action You Can Take, Increasing Your Internal Control & Happiness:

Which Strategy/Action Can You Truly Commit to Accomplishing This Week?

Visualize: How Will it Feel to Accomplish it?

Visualize: What Will it Cost You if You Don't?

Set a Date to Celebrate:

READING FOR INSPIRATION:

The Great Game of Business
and anything by Jack Stack & Bo Burlingham

Get in the Game
and anything by Steve Baker

Crucial Conversations
by Grenny, McMillan et al

Creating Competitive Advantage
by Jaynie L. Smith

Any Classics by:
- **Peter Drucker**
- **W. Edwards Deming**
- **Michael Porter**
- **Jim Collins**
- **Verne Harnish**
- **Patrick Lencioni**

13. QTR SYNERGY EXERCISE

The Whole is Greater Than the Sum of Its Parts

Aristotle
384–322 bce

Now that you have invested all the time and energy into the QTR Challenges, you will undoubtedly have several different things you want to accomplish in the next 90 days, rather than working on only one, then another, then another in succession.

This is when synergy comes into play. We're looking for 'two-fers' here. Your objective is to look for connections between different facets of your life that interact for an impact that is greater than working on any single one at a time.

We're looking for one activity that would affect several aspects of life. Heck, don't just look for 'two-fers', look for 'three-fers' or even 'four-fers'!

Let's try some on for size. One of my favorite things in the world is cooking with JoAnn during the holiday season. Okay, okay, before you judge me as some kind of Martha-Stewart-Currier-and-Ives-perfect-life bozo, let me admit to you that it doesn't happen too often. Mainly at holidays.

It's so fun because we'll have music playing, we're bumping into each other, laughing, smiling, just enjoying each other's company. There might even be a libation involved. But during the rest of the year, the kitchen is usually a solo enterprise. When the kids were all home, it was more of a factory.

What if we were to make cooking together more of an 'event' the rest of the year? We could impact multiple facets at the same time. Financially, we'd eat less restaurant and take-out food. Physically, we'd be eating better food in more reasonable portions. And wouldn't it give us time to build our relationship without the TV or internet stealing our attention from one another? There's a 'three-fer' right there!

What if I were to make walking three times a week a priority in my life? Physical, Mindset and even Spiritual could all see benefits. And if we did it together, that's a 'four-fer'! Amazing. Look at the examples, then use the four blanks for your brainstorming, but don't limit yourself. You may want to sketch out a dozen of these before you find something you want to commit to for the maximum impact in the next 90 days

QTR SYNERGY EXERCISE

EXAMPLE

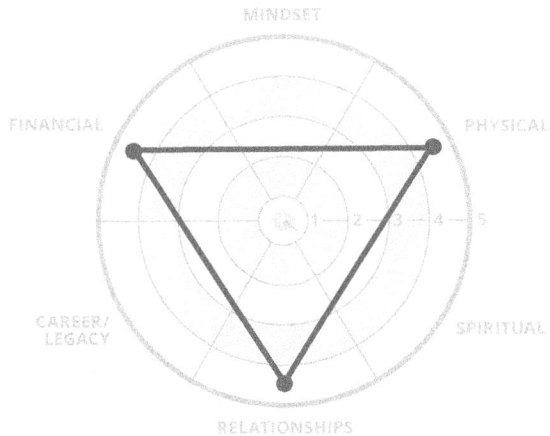

Cooking Together

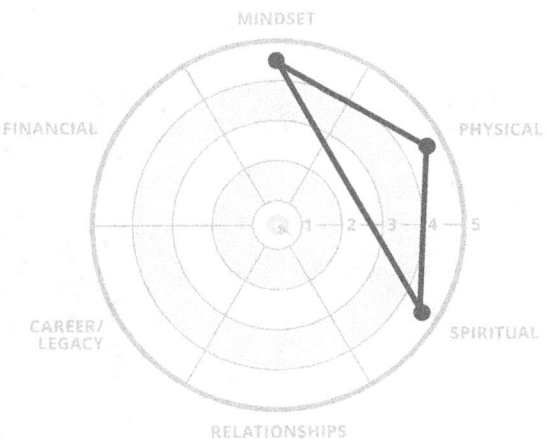

Walking 3x per Week

QTR SYNERGY EXERCISE

WORKSHEET

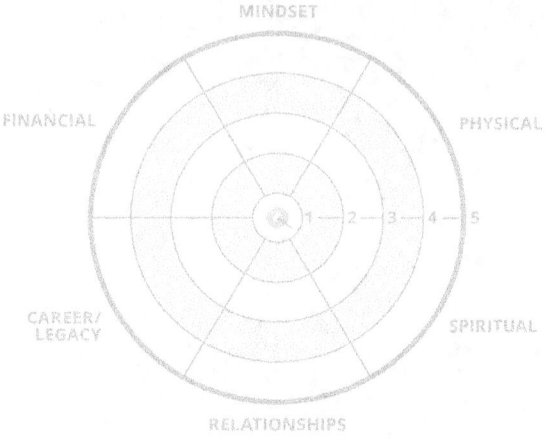

QTR SYNERGY EXERCISE

WORKSHEET

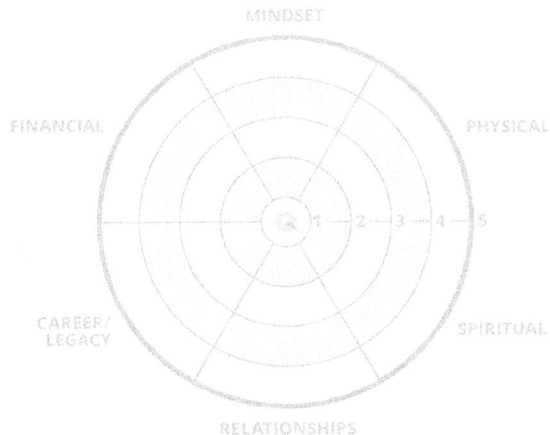

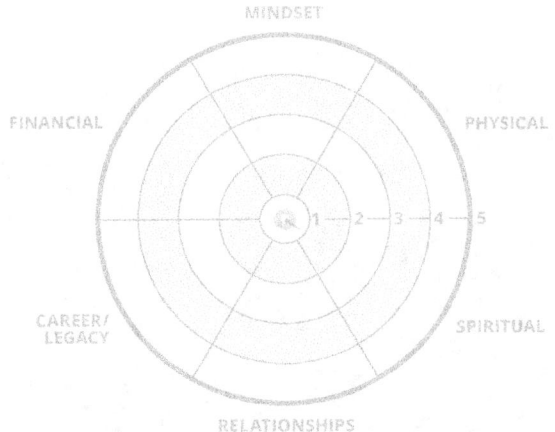

QTR Quality Time Remaining™

14. QTR 90 DAY ACTION PLAN

Life Is Too Short to Waste. Dreams Are Fulfilled Only Through Action, Not Through Endless Planning to Take Action.

David J. Schwartz
1927–1987

14. QTR 90 DAY ACTION PLAN

One of my all-time favorite quotes comes from *The Shawshank Redemption* when Andy Dufresne decides, "It comes down to one simple choice. Get busy livin' or get busy dyin'." It really captures the essence of Quality Time Remaining, doesn't it? Do you dream of absconding to Zihuatanejo, Mexico after you escape from your prison of personal autopilot? Make it your battle cry! We established early on that if you're not growing, you're decaying...so get busy livin'!

Bringing together everything you've been working on may be obvious to some, harder to pin down for others. Don't be afraid to go back and amend any one of the individual Challenges. As you synthesize the entire body of work you're creating, natural connections and synergies will emerge. What you're trying to do is accomplish as much positive change as you can with the least amount of effort. Remember 'minimum effective dose' and 'minimum viable product'?

Before you get started, a word about the 90-day time block. Through the years, I've actively sought out answers about human behavior, mostly to better understand why I do things the way that I do them. I am, if nothing else, a student of life.

If you read all the gurus, sages, and motivators, you can find decades of material on habits. Some scientific, some not so much. My personal philosophy is to find what works for you, no matter what the source. But when it comes to habits, everyone has an opinion. In fact, my new habit is to stop reading habits books and get to work.

> *"99% of failures come from people who have*
> *the habit of making excuses."*
> George Washington Carver
> *1864-1943*

The consensus seems to be that in order to rewire the neural pathways and cement a new behavior that will last is somewhere between six weeks and three months. What I can tell you from decades of coaching is that whatever you choose, the time block needs to be long enough to change behavior, short enough to be interesting. 90 days, seems to have a beautiful ring to it. Now, take some quiet time to review the work you've completed so far, and use it to build an amazing 90 Day Action Plan.

QTR 90 DAY ACTION PLAN

After Careful Reflection, Where are the Bright Spots in Your Life?

Which Facet of Life Holds Your Biggest Opportunity for Growth?

What is Your Top Goal in This Facet in the Next 90 Days?

Which Facet Holds Your Second Biggest Opportunity for Growth?

What is Your Top Goal in This Facet in the Next 90 Days?

Which Facet Holds Your Third Biggest Opportunity for Growth?

What is Your Top Goal in This Facet in the Next 90 Days?

What Synergy Have You Identified between these 3 Top Goals?

What Can you Commit to Accomplishing in 90 Days:

What Reward Will You Give Yourself?

Set a Date to Celebrate:

Signature:

15. QTR SUCCESS CHECKLIST

> **To Succeed, Work Hard, Never Give Up and Above All, Cherish a Magnificent Obsession.**
>
> Walt Disney
> *1901–1966*

If you just signed your 90 Day Action Plan, congratulations! You've done more than 97% of the United States population. According to a Harvard Study, only 3% of Americans have personal written goals. And you are 42% more likely to achieve them if they are indeed written down.

As part of the 3%, you're in rarefied air. How does that feel?

> *"In order to succeed, you must know what you are doing, like what you are doing, and believe in what you are doing."*
> *Will Rogers*
> *1879-1935*

Now it's all about execution. How will you prevent your 90 Day Action Plan from becoming another artifact in a file drawer or buried deep in your hard drive? Atul Gawande, author of *The Checklist Manifesto* writes, "Under conditions of complexity, not only are checklists a help, they are required for success."

If discipline and frequency are the secrets to QTR, accountability is the catalyst. Use this Checklist. Get a coach. Join a mastermind group. Tap a successful, accomplished friend to be your accountability buddy. Do whatever it takes to successfully fight your old habits and programming. You'll have to overcome your limiting beliefs.

Remember why you are doing this.

Remember that you're doing this for *you*.

Remember it will be good enough.

Remember that you're worth it.

QTR SUCCESS CHECKLIST

☐ I calculated my QTR.

☐ I used the 10 Year Timeline Assessment to identify critical milestones in my life.

☐ I used the Default Future Assessment to honestly assess critical issues in the next 1, 5, and 10 years.

☐ I used the Preferred Future Assessment to identify critical goals for myself in the next 1, 5, and 10 years.

☐ I assessed where in my life I am in growth and where I'm in decay.

☐ I assessed where I feel out of control in my life.

☐ I dug deep to identify and isolate the limiting beliefs and self-sabotaging behaviors that divert me from a feeling of control in my life.

☐ I have taken time to accurately rate each facet of my life, based on my feelings of control & happiness.

☐ I asked myself, "Am I fighting for what really matters most in this facet of my life?"

☐ I identified one action (that I can earnestly commit to) that will increase my internal control & happiness.

☐ I asked myself, "Considering the time I have left, does this really improve or degrade my quality of life in the long run?"

☐ I thoughtfully looked for synergies between possible actions I can take to compound my impact on multiple facets of my life.

☐ I set appointments in my calendar and sincerely committed to myself to execute over the next 90 days.

☐ Before I began my 90-day action plan, I pre-scheduled a date and a reward to celebrate my progress and growth.

☐ I consistently tracked, measured, and recorded my progress daily, and reviewed it weekly.

☐ I was diligent in recognizing and documenting all manifestations of resistance, procrastination, and self-sabotage throughout the 90 days.

☐ I read and listened to resources that kept me inspired and energized.

☐ I identified the bright spots, recognized the miracles, and celebrated my wins, and revisited my QTR materials to plan my next 90 days of growth.

16. THE QTR REDBOOK

**Expect the Best.
Prepare for the Worst.
Capitalize on What Comes.**

Zig Ziglar
1926–2012

16. THE QTR REDBOOK

The original QTR draft was completed on November 28th, 2022. Four days later, on December 1st, my kid brother Chris died in his sleep at the age of 54.

I'm not making this up for effect.

Yes, Chris had health problems, but by all accounts, he was on the upswing. To be clear, I did not write QTR because of my brother. Nor am I suggesting that the timing of his passing was some sort of universal sign that I was doing the right thing by writing the book.

It is my belief that in this life, if you're not actively designing it yourself, life is being designed *for you*, and life will happen *to* you.

When we went to Kansas City to see how we could help, we learned that Chris had left no documentation, no will, power of attorney, healthcare directive, or funeral arrangements. No one knew his phone code, his email password or bank account pin.

Nothing.

Just sit with that for a moment.

Losing Chris was terribly hard, but I can only imagine how hard it was for my parents, who were 88 at the time. Not only were they grieving the loss of a child but also dealing with the disposition of a lot of...well...stuff. It seems that dealing with all his property stretched their grieving process far beyond what they should have had to endure.

On our way home from Kansas City, JoAnn turned to me in the car and said, "You can't die. I wouldn't know where to begin..." Even though we'd created our own "Redbook" (our emergency readiness notebook) years earlier, she knew how hard it would be to make decisions and get things done while in a deep state of grief.

No. I did not write QTR because of Chris' death. But it was losing Chris that inspired me to add *The Redbook* to *Quality Time Remaining*.

The trouble with planning for your own passing is that few people want to talk about it, much less do it. Remember *premeditatio malorum*? This ancient Stoic practice of worst-case scenario planning makes you more resilient to life's inevitable setbacks. *The Redbook* is taking that practice to the next level.

WHAT INSPIRED THE REDBOOK: THE MOSCOW – WASHINGTON HOTLINE

People of my generation remember the Moscow-Washington Hotline, the direct line of communication set up between the U.S. and Soviet Union in 1962 after the Cuban Missile Crisis. It was designed to provide instant communication directly between heads of state to eliminate the possibility of accidental nuclear war. It was depicted in Stanley Kubrick's *Doctor Strangelove* as a bright red telephone (which is fascinating, as the film is black and white) and that image was forever imprinted on our minds. Thanks, Hollywood.

In real life, the Hotline has never even been a telephone. In the early days it was teletype machines, then faxes, then encrypted satellite email. And in over 60 years of service, it's still tested hourly, but rarely used. Still, the idea of an Emergency Hotline Red Phone has stuck with me my entire life.

As my prostatectomy surgery date approached, I was planning for the worst and expecting the best. This approach has served me well through the years and gives me a peace of mind that's hard to describe.

However, JoAnn doesn't see things the same way I do. You may have this same situation at home. While she wants all this 'hard to think about stuff' ready and accessible, doing it makes her uneasy. Her peace of mind comes from knowing that it's *done*.

I needed something that could be easily located in an emergency, like the Hotline. It would need to contain all of the contacts needed in an emergency such as attorneys, accountants, work and family contacts, as well as crucial documents like insurance policies, wills, powers of attorney, etc. Everything JoAnn would need if things went south.

A thin red three-ring binder was just the ticket, as it stood out when you opened our fire safe. This became affectionately known as our "Redbook". This binder allowed me to put everything necessary together and file it away. We only need to review it once a year to make sure everything is up to date. Then back it goes into the fire safe.

WHY YOUR REDBOOK IS IMPORTANT

If you were to die tomorrow, what would be the impact on your loved ones? I'm not trying to lay a guilt trip on you. According to Gallup Research, less than half of Americans have a will, much less a durable power of attorney for finance or healthcare. Gallup states that when it comes to our young, lower income or non-white Americans, that number drops to less than a third. In the U.S., we're as illiterate about estate planning as we are about money.

It's more about illiteracy and ignorance than it is about access. While I'd recommend using an attorney, today you can create a will for free in numerous ways. Your employer may provide an EAP (Employee Assistance Program) and there are numerous free online templates. You can even contact your state bar association to find pro-bono or judicare programs in your area.

To make this more approachable, think of planning ahead as less for you and more for those you leave behind. When *your* QTR is up, you'll have an unbelievable impact on the Quality Time Remaining of those you love most.

Face it. It's gonna happen, and probably not on your timeline. Mick Jagger once said, "I'd rather be dead than sing 'Satisfaction' when I'm 45." See what I mean? Might be sooner, might be later. But either way, none of us gets out alive.

Consider this a way to start an important plan to mitigate the stress and burden with which your bereaved family would otherwise be dealing. Not to mention reducing the amount that probate, the IRS, and others might come after.

If you've experienced the death of someone close, it's a time of emotion, confusion, and exhaustion. Every instruction, every direction can be a godsend to those left to deal with things. Use the *Redbook* as 'prompts' to get started. In creating your own *Redbook*, you may need additional copies of certain forms. Please make all the copies you need. But, if your friend wants to create a *Redbook*, tell them to buy their own damn copy.

There is a growing collection of books and programs that can help you think through how you'll leave things. Some have entertaining titles, like *Nobody Wants Your Sh*t* and *The Gentle Art of Swedish Death Cleaning*. If things like these help you get through the process, use them.

I promise you that your peace of mind will get a significant boost, and years from now, a lot of people will be very, very thankful.

> *"If you live each day as if it was your last, someday you'll most certainly be right."*
> *Steve Jobs*
> *1955-2011*

IMPORTANT: This is not a legal document, nor is it intended to be. But if you complete it, your legal fees may be significantly reduced because you'll be ready to have an attorney prepare the appropriate documents, as your wishes will be outlined and thought through.

16. The QTR Redbook

REDBOOK ESSENTIALS

Your Full Legal Name:

Address:

Mobile Phone:

Home Phone:

E-mail Address - Personal:

Occupation/Employer:

Business Address:

Business Phone:

E-mail Address - Business:

Social Security Number:

Date of Birth:

Age:

U.S. citizen?

Notes:

SPOUSE/PARTNER

Spouse/Partner's Full Legal Name:

Address:

Mobile Phone:

Home Phone:

E-mail Address - Personal:

Occupation/Employer:

Business Address:

Business Phone:

E-mail Address - Business:

Social Security Number:

Date of Birth:

Age:

U.S. citizen?

Notes:

MARITAL STATUS

Married/Single/Divorced

If married:

Date of Marriage:

Location of Marriage:

Previously Married?

If so, provide details and gather documents from that event.

NOTES

CHILDREN AND OTHER FAMILY

Full Legal Name:

Address:

Mobile Phone:

Home Phone:

E-mail Address - Personal:

Occupation/Employer:

Business Address:

Business Phone:

E-mail Address - Business:

Social Security Number:

Date of Birth:

Age:

U.S. citizen?

Was this child adopted?

Was this child from a previous marriage?

Does this child have any issues or concerns that need to be taken into consideration? (physical, mental, legal, financial, personal, marital)

CHILDREN AND OTHER FAMILY

Full Legal Name:

Address:

Mobile Phone:

Home Phone:

E-mail Address - Personal:

Occupation/Employer:

Business Address:

Business Phone:

E-mail Address - Business:

Social Security Number:

Date of Birth:

Age:

U.S. citizen?

Was this child adopted?

Was this child from a previous marriage?

Does this child have any issues or concerns that need to be taken into consideration? (physical, mental, legal, financial, personal, marital)

CHILDREN AND OTHER FAMILY

Full Legal Name:

Address:

Mobile Phone:

Home Phone:

E-mail Address - Personal:

Occupation/Employer:

Business Address:

Business Phone:

E-mail Address - Business:

Social Security Number:

Date of Birth:

Age:

U.S. citizen?

Was this child adopted?

Was this child from a previous marriage?

Does this child have any issues or concerns that need to be taken into consideration? (physical, mental, legal, financial, personal, marital)

CHILDREN AND OTHER FAMILY

Full Legal Name:

Address:

Mobile Phone:

Home Phone:

E-mail Address - Personal:

Occupation/Employer:

Business Address:

Business Phone:

E-mail Address - Business:

Social Security Number:

Date of Birth:

Age:

U.S. citizen?

Was this child adopted?

Was this child from a previous marriage?

Does this child have any issues or concerns that need to be taken into consideration? (physical, mental, legal, financial, personal, marital)

RELATIVES

Living Members of Immediate Family

(if none, nearest living relatives)

Full Legal Name

Relationship

Address

Phone

Notes:

RELATIVES

Living Members of Immediate Family

(if none, nearest living relatives)

Full Legal Name

Relationship

Address

Phone

Notes:

RELATIVES

Living Members of Immediate Family

(if none, nearest living relatives)

Full Legal Name

Relationship

Address

Phone

Notes:

RELATIVES

Living Members of Immediate Family

(if none, nearest living relatives)

Full Legal Name

Relationship

Address

Phone

Notes:

IMPORTANT DOCUMENTS

Last Will and Testament

Trust Agreement

Durable Power of Attorney – Financial

Durable Power of Attorney – Healthcare

Health Care Directive/Living Will

Other important documents:

(Pre-nuptial agreement, Divorce decree, etc)

KEY ADVISORS - ACCOUNTANT

Accountant/CPA:

Firm:

Name:

Address:

Mobile Phone:

Business Phone:

E-mail Address:

KEY ADVISORS - BANK

Bank Contact:

Institution:

Name:

Address:

Mobile Phone:

Business Phone:

E-mail Address:

Account Number(s):

KEY ADVISORS - INSURANCE

Insurance Agent:

Firm:

Name:

Address:

Mobile Phone:

Business Phone:

E-mail Address:

Policy Number(s):

KEY ADVISORS - INVESTMENT

Investment Broker/Financial Advisor:

Firm:

Name:

Address:

Mobile Phone:

Business Phone:

E-mail Address:

Account Number(s):

KEY ADVISORS - PHYSICIAN

Physician(s):

Practice:

Name:

Address:

Mobile Phone:

Business Phone:

E-mail Address:

EMR Number(s):

KEY ADVISORS - PHYSICIAN

Physician(s):

Practice:

Name:

Address:

Mobile Phone:

Business Phone:

E-mail Address:

EMR Number(s):

KEY ADVISORS - PHYSICIAN

Physician(s):

Practice:

Name:

Address:

Mobile Phone:

Business Phone:

E-mail Address:

EMR Number(s):

DIGITAL FOOTPRINT

List all devices, including computers, phones, tablets, and smart devices.

List all email accounts, subscriptions, and memberships.

Include the username, password, and security questions for each account.

Do you have specific instructions on how these digital assets should be shared, closed, or destroyed?

MILITARY SERVICE

DD-214:

Service Number:

Do you have a pension?

Do you have service-connected disability?

Notes:

Note: Be prepared to gather and discuss any other items of consequence when you meet with your estate planning professionals. This may include trusts, gifts, inheritances, community property etc.

PROPERTY - REAL ESTATE

Property Address:

Property Ownership (Joint or Individual):

Property Type:

(primary residence, second home, land, commercial, rental)

Mortgage:

PROPERTY - VEHICLE

Vehicle (autos, motorcycles, watercraft, aircraft, trailers, etc):

Make:

Model:

Year:

VIN:

Loan:

Notes:

PROPERTY - VEHICLE

Vehicle (autos, motorcycles, watercraft, aircraft, trailers, etc):

Make:

Model:

Year:

VIN:

Loan:

Notes:

PROPERTY - VEHICLE

Vehicle (autos, motorcycles, watercraft, aircraft, trailers, etc):

Make:

Model:

Year:

VIN:

Loan:

Notes:

PROPERTY - VEHICLE

Vehicle (autos, motorcycles, watercraft, aircraft, trailers, etc):

Make:

Model:

Year:

VIN:

Loan:

Notes:

BANK ACCOUNTS

Institution:

Name:

Address:

Mobile Phone:

Business Phone:

E-mail Address:

Type of Account:

Account Number(s):

BANK ACCOUNTS

Institution:

Name:

Address:

Mobile Phone:

Business Phone:

E-mail Address:

Type of Account:

Account Number(s):

BANK ACCOUNTS

Institution:

Name:

Address:

Mobile Phone:

Business Phone:

E-mail Address:

Type of Account:

Account Number(s):

SAFE DEPOSIT BOX

Location:

Number:

Location of key:

Location:

Number:

Location of key:

FINANCIAL SECURITIES

Security Type:

Institution:

Ownership (Joint or Individual):

Account Number(s):

Contact:

Notes:

FINANCIAL SECURITIES

Security Type:

Institution:

Ownership (Joint or Individual):

Account Number(s):

Contact:

Notes:

RETIREMENT ACCOUNTS

Company:

Type of Plan:

Ownership (Joint or Individual):

Beneficiaries:

Account Number(s):

Contact:

RETIREMENT ACCOUNTS

Company:

Type of Plan:

Ownership (Joint or Individual):

Beneficiaries:

Account Number(s):

Contact:

INSURANCE POLICY

Agent:

Firm:

Name:

Address:

Mobile Phone:

Business Phone:

E-mail Address:

Beneficiaries:

Policy Number(s):

Notes:

INSURANCE POLICY

Agent:

Firm:

Name:

Address:

Mobile Phone:

Business Phone:

E-mail Address:

Beneficiaries:

Policy Number(s):

Notes:

INSURANCE POLICY

Agent:

Firm:

Name:

Address:

Mobile Phone:

Business Phone:

E-mail Address:

Beneficiaries:

Policy Number(s):

Notes:

INTELLECTUAL PROPERTY

Property:

Include any documentation of patent, copyright, or trademark ownership that may have value.

Notes:

INTELLECTUAL PROPERTY

Property:

Include any documentation of patent, copyright, or trademark ownership that may have value.

Notes:

BUSINESS OWNERSHIP

Business Name:

Type of Business:

Ownership Interest:

Address:

Key Contact:

Mobile Phone:

Business Phone:

E-mail Address:

BUSINESS OWNERSHIP

Business Name:

Type of Business:

Ownership Interest:

Address:

Key Contact:

Mobile Phone:

Business Phone:

E-mail Address:

PERSONAL PROPERTY

Personal Effects:

Jewelry:

Firearms:

Art/Antiques:

PERSONAL PROPERTY

Furnishings:

Collectibles/Memorabilia:

Other Valuables:

YOUR WISHES & INSTRUCTIONS

This section is important as it will help direct the disposition of your estate after your death. Use these writing prompts to prepare for discussions with your estate planning professionals. If you've already prepared a will, some of the questions will already be answered.

What would you like to happen to your estate?

Who do wish to appoint as your Personal Representative?

Who do wish to receive your property, when and how?

Who should care for any minor children?

What instructions will the caretaker need?

Who should care for any pets?

What instructions will the caretaker need?

GIFTS

Are there any gifts you wish to make?

Family

Individuals

Charities

Describe how you would like your funeral to be arranged:

Disposition of your remains, memorial service, burial/internment?

Any anatomical donations?

17. BRINGING IT ALL TOGETHER

It Comes Down to One Simple Choice. Get Busy Livin', or Get Busy Dyin'.

Andy Dufresne
1917–????

Congratulations! You've taken your first steps in creating a life of your design.

I hope that the QTR process has helped you figure out who you are, what you want, and how you intend to get it in the time you have left, no matter your age.

You have embraced your mortality, gotten objective about what you'll do with the time you have, you've chosen growth over decay, and you've learned that you must become accepting of your own happiness and satisfaction.

If you've completed the Challenges earnestly, then looked for synergies and identified just a few things to work on in the next 90 days, then you have a plan! As you work your Action Plan, you'll feel a sense of purpose, accomplishment, and satisfaction you may have been missing for years.

And if you have the guts to do it, drafting your own *Redbook* will give you a peace of mind the vast majority of people will *never feel in their lifetime*.

Making a living sucks. Designing a life is freeing. And that, my friends, is exactly what Quality Time Remaining is all about. Now that you know how long the game may last, don't you think it'll change how you play? I hope so.

> *"Having a strong sense of controlling one's life is a more dependable predictor of positive feelings of well-being than any of the objective conditions of life we have considered."*
> *Angus Campbell*
> *1910-1980*

I wish you all the best as you make your own luck, determine your own happiness, and level up your quality of life with the people you love... in the time you have left.

Enjoy your journey, and make the most of your Quality Time Remaining!

18. ACKNOWLEDGMENTS

This book would not have been possible without the support of an amazing community of friends. With deep appreciation, I'd like to thank Howard Partridge, Jeff Evenson, Kristin Binford, Rich Armstrong, Will "The Actuary" Brabson, Madi Baker, Colin Baker, Michele & Darin Bridges, Cheri Perry, Victor Aspengren, John Williams, Chris Shaefer, Janet Livingston, Kristi Stringer, Doug Hague, Jack O'Riley, Kermit Engh, Brian Underhill, Chris Shelden, Adam Trebelo, Charlotte Eckley, Breana Murphy, and Liz Wilder.

Very special thanks to Jack Stack, Dennis Sheppard, and Krisi Schell at SRC Holdings Corporation and my team at The Great Game of Business, Inc. for believing in me and having the vision to support the QTR project.

19. ABOUT THE AUTHOR

Steve Baker is a top-rated author, speaker and coach on business, leadership, and employee engagement. He has been coaching high-growth business owners to achieve financial results and cultural change for over 20 years.

Steve co-authored 2 seminal books on open-book management and business literacy; *Get in the Game: How to Create Rapid Financial Results and Lasting Cultural Change*, and the 20th anniversary update of the number one bestseller, *The Great Game of Business*. What he's done for business literacy, Steve now does for life & longevity literacy.

Through the years, he discovered a universal truth, in both billionaires and frontline workers alike. Top performers typically give their very best to their work life, leaving their personal lives with the leftovers.

His latest work, *QTR: Quality Time Remaining*™, is fulfilling his objective in life – having fun helping people design and live their best life in the time they have left.

His audiences range from Harvard and MIT to the Department of Defense. Steve is on the faculty of the Growth Institute, and a frequent speaker for high-performance groups including Entrepreneurs' Organization (EO), YPO, Vistage Worldwide, and INC 5000.

When he's not on the road, Steve is a banned, but award-winning artist and spends his own Quality Time Remaining with his trophy wife, JoAnn, their three above-average children, and their Sig-O's.

20. WORK WITH QTR

BOOKS AND RESOURCES

Visit QTRbook.com for additional copies of Quality Time Remaining and the latest resources from QTR.

KEYNOTES AND WORKSHOPS

Steve Baker engages an audience and delivers more actionable takeaways than any speaker you'll see this year. (Plus, he's the easiest to work with.) Let Steve make you *and* your audience the hero by booking at steve@qtrbook.com.

COACHING

QTR accepts only a handful of one-on-one coaching clients each year. To apply, contact steve@qtrbook.com.

MEDIA INQUIRIES

For media inquiries or interviews, please email steve@qtrbook.com. We promise to respond promptly.